This book was printed on 100% chlorine-free bleached paper in accordance with the TCF standard.

EVERGREEN is an imprint of Benedikt Taschen Verlag GmbH

© for this edition: 1997 Benedikt Taschen Verlag GmbH
Hohenzollernring 53, D–50672 Köln
© 1988 ATELIER D´ÉDITION «LE SEPTIÈME FOU», Geneva
Illustrations, layout and conception: Michel Saudan and Sylvia Saudan-Skira, Geneva
Text: Michel Melot
Translation: Anthea Bell in association with First Edition Translations Ltd., Cambridge, UK
Cover: Mark Thomson, London

Printed in Italy
ISBN 3-8228-8256-9
GB

CHÂTEAUX
OF THE
LOIRE

MICHEL MELOT

EVERGREEN

CONTENTS

1 7 THE LANDSCAPE

10 The river: The Loire and its embankments
12 The hillsides
14 The tributaries:
 14 *The Loir and the Cher*
 16 *The Vienne and the Indre*
18 Building materials:
 18 *Timber from the oak forests*
 20 *Timberwork*
 22 *The limestone of Touraine*
 24 *The slate of Angers*
 26 *Variegated brickwork*
28 A mosaic of building materials
30 The château in its setting

2 35 THE HERITAGE

40 The inaccessible château
42 The defensive wall
44 The ramparts
46 The keep
48 The moat
50 The drawbridge
52 Parapet walks and machicolations

3 55 THE NEW KINGS

60 The manors of René d'Anjou
62 Royal architecture and bourgeois architecture
64 The royal châteaux:
 64 *Loches*
 66 *Amboise*
68 Louis XII at Blois
70 Architecture opening up to new policies
72 Transitional areas
74 The austere "residence" of an itinerant court
76 The queen's household
78 From austerity to magnificence
80 The gardens
82 Decoration in the Italian style
84 Chambord, a château built to charm and inspire awe

4 87 THE NEW LORDS

92 The town mansion
94 Built on the royal model
96 Country houses and town houses
98 A new style of ornamentation in prosperous cities
100 Refinement: The private town house
102 The Hôtel de Ville: An expression of power

5   105   AZAY-LE-RIDEAU, A MODEL
     110   The approach to Azay-le-Rideau
     112   The plan of the château with its angle towers
     114   The organization of the façade
     116   The design
     118   The staircase
     122   Ornamentation of the doors and window frames
     124   The dormers
     126   The roofs

6   129   VARIATIONS
     134   The new organizing principle: Balance
     136   The underlining of form
     138   Ornamentation accentuating the structure
     140   The importance of the staircase
         142   *The staircase as motive force*
         144   *The straight staircase*
         146   *The staircase as backdrop*
     148   The last outcrop of chivalry:
         The lantern at Chambord
     150   The influence of Pavia
     152   Flamboyant decor
     154   A taste for antiquity
     156   Cornices
     158   The emblematic function of dormers

7   161   THE NEW MASTERS
     166   Feudal nostalgia
     168   The new owners:
         168   *The liberal aristocracy at Azay-le-Rideau*
         170   *The new industrialists at Chenonceaux*
         172   *The alliance of aristocracy and finance at Chaumont*
     174   The royal residences and the state
     176   Restoration work
     178   Chambord and its park …
     180   … an echo of the Absolute

     184   MAP OF CHÂTEAUX
     187   HISTORICAL OVERVIEW
     189   NOTES
     191   SOURCES OF QUOTATIONS
     193   BIBLIOGRAPHY
     197   INDEX
     203   ILLUSTRATIONS

I

THE LANDSCAPE

Of the châteaux of the Loire, we see little more today than their steep slate roofs and harmonious façades of pale stonework gilded by the light of Touraine. We might confine ourselves to that perspective, basking in their beauty and an undiscriminating sense of nostalgia. Instead, we shall search for their true nature elsewhere. We shall not have far to look. For they were built as instruments of oppression; their beauty was a means of inspiring deference; they were, in short, as manifestations of the power and authority of new wealth – an authority that their owners sought to impose on the three orders of the kingdom and on each other. And so we may also read in them the rise, ambition and fall of their various owners. These are the themes that we shall pursue amid the pleasant landscapes and fertile soils where they were built.

The basin of the middle Loire, between Orléans and Angers, and in particular the valleys of the Loire, the Cher and the Indre are extraordinarily rich in châteaux. There are historical reasons for this, but landscape and situation have also been important. These valleys have been trading routes since prehistoric times, and the Loire valley became a highway for communication between the Mediterranean and the Atlantic. Digoin and Roanne, the highest navigable points on the Loire, are less than a hundred kilometres from Mâcon and Lyon, towns easily reached by road. As early as Gallo-Roman times the boatmen of the rivers Saône and Loire had formed a powerful corporation.[1] Passengers wishing to travel to Paris would disembark at Orléans, which consequently became a major commercial centre. The importance of this axis increased when Renaissance France succumbed to the lure of Italy and attempted its conquest. The discovery of the Americas gave new meaning to the Atlantic seaboard and brought wealth to the port of Nantes.

With the three hubs of trade – Paris, Nantes and Lyon – prospering within easy reach, François I might well note how fortuitously the Loire flowed "through all the best towns and countryside from Lyon to Brittany".[2] Strabo had long since observed that the cities reflected in its waters were arranged as though by intelligent foresight".[3]

This network of navigable waterways passing through fertile land also provided suitable sites for settlement. Most of the large châteaux stand at the water's edge. Sometimes they are porched on rocky spurs created by confluences, of which there are many; for instance, at Amboise where the Amasse meets the Loire, or at Blois where the Loire meets the Arrou. Sometimes they stand on prominences lacking natural defences but of great strategic importance, as the etymology of their names suggests: Montbazon, Montrésor, Montrichard. Sometimes they cling to a chalky cliff or a hillside above a valley, like the châteaux of Chinon on the Vienne, Ussé on the Indre and Chaumont on the Loire. Occasionally, they were built on islands, as at l'Ile-Bouchard on the Vienne or Azay-le-Rideau on the Indre. Sometimes a part of the river's flow was diverted around a château, creating a moat and means of access. Leonardo da Vinci planned to draw on the Sauldre in this way to defend the châteaux he was to build for François I at Romorantin; this project inspired the diversion of the Cosson at Chambord.[4]

The tributaries of the Loire form a dense network of subsidiary waterways, whose many staging posts and fords gave rise to prosperous communities. The Cher, Indre and Vienne were convenient, economical routes for transporting travellers, soldiers, provisions and building materials. The many large rivers and their smaller tributaries thus became lines of communication favouring agriculture and commerce, and people settled along their banks. Without waterborne transport, the silkworks of Tours founded by Louis XI could not have employed 20,000 workers in the sixteenth century; the *Boutique du roi*, which provided the princely courts with weapons and clothing, would not have made the fifteenth-century financier Jacques Coeur and his successors wealthy so soon; and Charles VIII and Louis XII could not have reached Milan so quickly.

In April 1519, when the foundations of Azay-le-Rideau were being laid, the accounts record payment "to the bargees who brought stone and sand from Bourré and St-Aignan to the building site, navigating from the valley of the Cher to the valley of the Indre". Similarly, the stone to build Chambord was brought from the quarries of Bourré and Lye on the banks of the Cher.[5] The river was the natural route for the limestone of Touraine, which was such a gift to the masons; the chalky Bourré stone, soft and easy to build into courses of large stone blocks, and the harder limestone of St-Aignan, ideal for sculptural decoration. But for its limestone, Touraine would not, at such an early date, have seen the soaring ten-foot span of the semi-circular Romanesque vaults at Saumur, or the great walls of its castle keeps, thirty-six metres in height at Beaugency and thirty-seven metres at Loches.

Slate from Angers, cut at Trélazé where the Armorican schist lies in thin, even layers came up the Loire on convoys of flat-bottomed barges called *gabares*. These boats went downstream on the strong current, and their triangular sails carried them back upstream before the onshore wind. The watermen of the Loire formed a strong corporation, which had its headquarters in Orléans. They had to pass 200 toll stations on the way from Nantes to Roanne, and either paid toll in kind from their cargo or took advantage of the free passage allowed to slate by calling out three times, *"Je meyne ardoise"* ["I am carrying slate"][6], and throwing a few slates into the water as confirmation.

Roger Dion has written that "the rôle of the Loire and its major tributaries was not so much to shape the relief of the area as to determine the nature of the soil".[7] It is true that the Loire, which flows only through soft terrain, spreads out into a wide, indefinite and generally straight river-bed. Water can easily find a course in soil of this kind, and the clay beneath the limestone will hold it: there are many springs, and settlement was possible throughout the region. Fine oak forests grow around the plateaux, which rise only slightly above the valleys, and provided game and timber in addition to the already abundant resources of the area. The forests of Blois, Loches and Chinon were a source of timber for beams and planks, and for the great roof beams of the vaulting still present, almost intact, at Blois and in the little château of Fougères-sur-Bièvre near the forest. Well supplied as it was with sand, slate, various kinds of limestone, and timber from its oaks, and with many waterways at its disposal, the Loire valley seemed ideally suited to castle-building.

Since the Loire makes its meandering way along a very soft and changeable course, a decision was taken in the time of Henry Plantagenet, Comte d'Anjou (King Henry II of England) to contain it with dykes. These structures were intended to protect the fertile land inundated every spring; the land could then be occupied by small but profitable farms. These embankments or ramparts, known in French as *levées* and *turcies* and built by the forced labour of generations of serfs, have shaped banks of the Loire almost throughout the whole of its course.[8] However, the construction of the *levées* achieved something more than its original agricultural purpose; the fertility of the soil was soon less important than the boom in trade and urban development. They quickly became a roadway along the river rather than a rampart to contain it, and when Louis XI gave orders for their extension between

Nicolas Tassin
Plans et profils de toutes les principales villes ... de France
Amboise
Paris, 1631

Blois and Tours, the aim was not so much to acquire new arable land and populate new villages as to provide a convenient road link between the towns of the region, now among the busiest in the kingdom. Modern roads long followed the same route, running parallel to the river, and in more than one place these embankments carried the railways which put an end to river navigation after 1850. Thanks to this transport network, geographically predetermined and enhanced by civil engineering, the bourgeois urban society created by the early industrial and commercial revolution found all that it needed already present in the basin of the Loire.

The fertile alluvial deposits of the many valleys of the Loire region make excellent soil for valuable crops such as fruit, vegetables and flowers, and the court and the prosperous urban middle classes provided an ever-growing market for them. This agricultural specialization explains the title "Garden of France" bestowed on the Loire valley by Rabelais. It was quoted in the first extant guide to the roads of France, which dates from the middle of the sixteenth century. Indeed, Italian influence was more strongly felt in the gardens than in the architecture of France.[9] Charles VIII had been captivated by the culture of Italy, and gardeners were among the first artists and craftsmen that he "imported". They included Pacello da Mercogliano, who was commissioned to redesign the gardens of Amboise and Blois. Imported plants included melons and artichokes, grown along with such already famous specialities of the Loire valley as asparagus, prunes, grapes for the wines of Orléans and pears, not forgetting that amber-coloured plum, the *reine-claude*, which owes its name to Queen Claude of France, wife of François I.

Between Tours and Chinon, the valleys of the Vienne, the Indre and the Cher join the valley of the Loire in a series of confluences which make a rich region particularly fertile. The area produces an abundance of industrial and food crops including hemp, fruit and vegetables. It is a region of small farms that used to be worked by hand, on soil where a couple of hectares were enough to keep a family. These farms lie in the *varennes*, "wild or waste land" formerly used for hunting, where, on the edge of broad river valleys, the alluvial soils extend beyond the flood plain. When well cultivated, the *varennes* are almost as fertile as the river meadows. Beyond the *varennes* are plateaux, such as the wide Sainte-Maure plateau between the rivers Indre and Vienne. Here the arable land is poorer and the landscape more austere, with moorland, and, towards the Berry, heather-rich heathland.

In this region of small, prosperous proprietors, the owner of the local château was not necessarily a large landowner, as was so often the case in other parts of France. The lord of the manor had to be able to defend the scattered independent peasants, but he was not economically dominant. As a result, this region was never subjected by a few great feudal overlords. The master here was the king himself, and the owners of châteaux in the sixteenth century were frequently court officials, enriched by commerce and finance, who had close connections with the city and occasionally with the local countryside. The château itself was a symbol of such a man's status, his country house and if necessary a fortified refuge in times of trouble. Most important of all, however, the feudal and manorial system, though it had now fallen into disuse, reinforced his claim upon the chivalric codes which constituted the only justification for his tenuous and recently acquired power.

Conquest was easy in this landscape of low plateaux and shallow valleys, and it was all the more to be feared because wealth is a temptation, and the division of land into small plots left the peasants defenceless. The power of the château united and protected them, and in the absence of naturally rugged features in the landscape a stronghold was indispensable if the countryside was to be supervised, communication routes controlled, and enemies deterred or contained if they attacked. The châteaux of Touraine, almost all of them built on the sites of former fortresses, were at once obstacles and landmarks in an area desirable, strategic for trade and easily accessible, which seemed to invite conquest.

Nicolas Tassin
Plans et profils de toutes les principales villes … de France
Tours
Paris, 1631

The river: The Loire and its embankments

"… Travelling by the waterway
From Orléans to Blois one day,
I saw some ships that did not stay
But through the water cut their way,
Straight as its stream before them lay.
They sailed on lightly at their ease,
Having their will, which is to say
A free, a fair and favouring breeze…

Those ships I saw were blithe and gay,
While stormy grief made me delay.
I pray to God that he may please
At last to grant me on my way
A free, a fair and favouring breeze."

Charles d'Orléans (1394–1465), *Poésies*

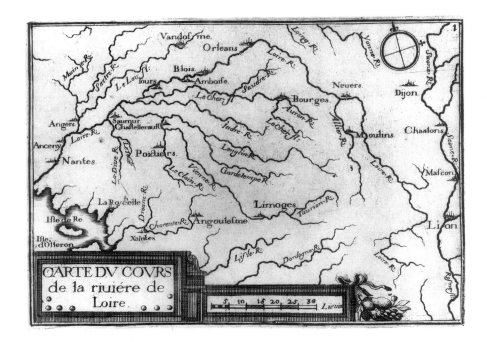

FACING PAGE ABOVE:
Nicolas Tassin
Plans et profils de toutes les principales villes … de France
Map of the course of the river Loire
Paris, 1631

The Loire
FACING PAGE BELOW:
Embankment between Amboise and Tours
ABOVE:
Former discharging wharf at Bréhémont

The hillsides

"… I looked eagerly for the much-vaunted sights of the Loire banks;
I saw nothing but little poplars and willows, not a tree so much as
sixty feet tall, not a single specimen of those fine oaks found in the
valley of the Arno, not one striking hill. Fertile meadows everywhere,
and a quantity of islands lying level with the water, overgrown with
a forest of young willows a dozen feet tall, their slender, drooping
branches trailing in the river. It was between these islands, verdant
but not picturesque, that the steamboat made its way. We often saw
the turrets of some Renaissance château standing five hundred feet
from the river."

Stendhal, *Mémoires d'un touriste*, 1838

FACING PAGE:
Château de Saumur
Late 14th century, built for Louis I, duc
d'Anjou, fortified in the 16th century
by Duplessis-Mornay

ABOVE:
Château de Chaumont
1465–1511, originally built
for Pierre d'Amboise
West wing

ABOVE:
St-Aignan (Loir-et-Cher)
Bridge over the Cher

LEFT:
Vendôme (Loir-et-Cher)
Bridge over an arm of the Loir

FACING PAGE:
Montrichard (Loir-et-Cher)
Bridge over the Cher

The tributaries: The Loir and the Cher

"…What pleasure is there living in the green
Vale of Bourgueil? The Muse was never seen
In Anjou; leave that place, come to Vendôme
Where tall trees raise their crowns to heaven's dome.
A thousand woods and plains their beauties show,
A hundred thousand springs of water flow,
While Echo from a thousand rocks around
Casts back my verse, and songs of love resound."

Pierre de Ronsard, *Le Voyage de Tours* in *Les Amours,* Book II, 1553

The Vienne and the Indre

"… These flat, sandy moors, casting a gloom over one's spirits for a distance of about a league, end in a coppice beside the road to Saché, the name of the parish to which Frapesle belongs. This road, leading to the Chinon highway well beyond Ballan, skirts an undulating plain without any distinguishing features until it reaches a little place called Artannes.

Here you come upon a valley which begins at Montbazon and ends at the Loire, and seems to bound along beneath the châteaux standing on the double crest of the hills: a magnificent emerald cup with the Indre winding its serpentine way along the bottom."

Honoré de Balzac, *Le Lys dans la Vallée*, 1839

FACING PAGE:
The Indre between Saché and
Pont-de-Ruan

LEFT:
The Indre near Rigny-Ussé

ABOVE:
The Vienne between l'Ile-Bouchard
and Chinon

Building materials: Timber from the oak forests

"… Near Blois there is a great forest over eleven leagues long
and four wide, containing several country houses built by
various kings: wild animals abound there, among others a deer
with horns no less marvellous than those of which I spoke
above, for which reason it is forbidden to course the creature,
and every respect is paid to it, such as one would show to a
wonder of the world."

Andrea Navagero, *Voyage d'André Navagero en Espagne et
en France,* 1528

FACING PAGE:
Chambord park (Loir-et-Cher)
Forest in autumn.

ABOVE:
Amboise (Indre-et-Loire)
Manor of Le Clos-Lucé, 1477
Post and beam of the gallery

LEFT:
Château de Fougères-sur-Bièvre
1475–1520, for Pierre de Refuge
Angle tower, timber structures of the turret

Timberwork

"…Woodman, ah woodman, hearken, stay your blow:
Those are no trees that you are laying low;
Do you not see the oozing of the blood
Of nymphs who dwelt within the living wood?

Forest, high house of woodland birds, no more
Shall stag or graceful roe-deer tread your floor,
Grazing beneath the shade of your green crown,
Where dappled sunlight through the leaves shines down."

Pierre de Ronsard, *Elégie sur la forêt de Gastine,* 1584

FACING PAGE:
Château de Fougères-sur-Bièvre
1475–1520, for Pierre de Refuge
Timber roof structures of the main building,
in the shape of an upturned hull

ABOVE:
Château de Blois
François I wing, 1515–pre-1524
Roof trusses; timber roof structures in the
shape of an upturned hull

The limestone of Touraine

"… However, the grandest and most picturesque feature of the Loire is a vast retaining wall of limestone mingled with sandstone, millstone grit and potter's clay which runs all along the right bank and which extends from Blois to Tours in an extraordinarily diverse and pleasing manner, sometimes wild and rocky, sometimes resembling an English garden with trees and flowers. It is crowned with ripening vines and smoking chimneys, and is as full of holes as a sponge and as densely populated as an anthill.

There are deep caverns here, once the dens of the forgers who counterfeited the E of the Tours mint and flooded the province with forged sous. Today the rugged mouths of these caves are closed by decorative window frames fitted into the rock, and now and then you see the graceful profile of a young girl in a curious sort of cap, engaged in packing aniseed, angelica and coriander into boxes. The confectioners have taken over from the forgers."

Victor Hugo, *En Voyage, Alpes et Pyrénées,* 1843

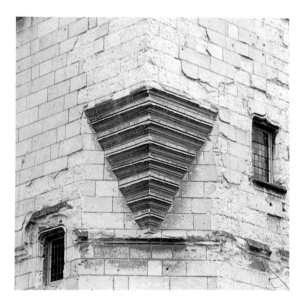

ABOVE:
Saumur (Maine-et-Loire)
15th-century Hôtel de Ville
Cul-de-lampe of an angle turret

RIGHT:
Trèves-Cunault (Maine-et-Loire)
Fortified farm, pendentive of the échauguette

The slate of Angers

"… Happy the man who at long last comes home
From a far voyage, like Ulysses bold
Or Jason who bore off the fleece of gold,
Wise and experienced, never more to roam.
When, alas, when shall I too see my own
Village with smoking chimneys, as of old?
My house and garden when shall I behold,
Dearer to me than any province known?

I love my own ancestral walls, my land,
Far more than Roman palaces with grand
Façades, fine slate better than marble fair,
More than the Tiber or the Palatine
The Lyré and the Loire, for they are mine:
I'll have no sea winds, but soft Anjou air."

Joachim du Bellay, *Les Regrets,* 1558

FACING PAGE:
Château de Blois
Roofs of the town, seen from the terrace

RIGHT:
Château d'Azay-le-Rideau,
1518–1527, for Gilles Berthelot
West roof, with chimneys

ABOVE:
Château de Blois
Louis XII wing, 1498–1504
Dormer window

LEFT:
Château de Fougères-sur-Bièvre,
1475–1520, for Pierre de Refuge
Roof of the main building,
with dormer window

LEFT:
Tours (Indre-et-Loire)
Hôtel de la Petite Bourdaisière
Detail of brickwork

Château du Moulin
1490–1506, for Philippe du Moulin

RIGHT:
Detail of south-east façade of the main building
FACING PAGE:
Lozenge and rectangle patterns on the south-west façade

Variegated brickwork

"…Why deprive ourselves of the use of enamelled terracotta in our palaces and châteaux, always furnishing their exteriors with those dressings of stone that look chilly and dismal, particularly in our climate? The judicious use of earthenware tiles, or even painted protective coatings in less exposed parts of the building, could save enough on stone to make up for any extra expense on these facings. The Renaissance architects of Italy and even France did not deny themselves the use of such resources, both decorative and economical, in their masonry, and they respected stone enough not to treat it with unnecessary prodigality."

Viollet-le-Duc, *Entretiens sur l'architecture,* 11th conversation, 1872

A mosaic of building materials

Château de Mortier-Crolles
late 15th century, built for Pierre de Rohan,
maréchal de Gié
Towers of the fortress seen from the moat

ABOVE:
Château des Réaux
West wing, built 1495–1559 for the
Briçonnet family
Main building, with entrance towers
and keep

ABOVE:
Château de Montpoupon
1320 for the de Prie family
Main building and entrance pavilion,
early 16th century

RIGHT:
The Vintage
French tapestry of c. 1500
Paris, Musée de Cluny

FACING PAGE:
Château de Montrésor
1493–late 16th century, for Imbert de
Bastarnay, seigneur de Bridoré
The seigneurial apartments, early 16th century

The château in its setting

"… Nothing is lacking; this is the heart of Touraine, the richest land
in all France. There is excellent pasture for the cattle, which provide
meat and dairy produce of high quality, the wines and fruit are the
best in France, and to these may be added wheat, timber and fodder.
The whole countryside is fertile and well cultivated, with many shady
groves: fruitfulness here unites with pleasure. Fish comes not only
from the rivers but also from the sea, and is brought from Nantes,
not far away."

Jérôme Lippomano, *Voyage de Jérôme Lippomano,* 1577

ABOVE:
Château du Coudray-Montpensier
1380–late 15th century, for Louis I d'Anjou
View from the hillsides of Seuilly

BELOW:
Return from the Hunt
French tapestry of c. 1500
Paris, Musée de Cluny

FACING PAGE:
Château d'Ussé
2nd half of 15th century–1535, for Jean V
de Bueil and the d'Espinay family
View of the north façade

"… Do you know that region called the Garden of France, where you breathe pure air amidst verdant plains watered by a great river? If you have travelled through the beautiful landscape of Touraine in the summer months you will have followed the tranquil Loire for a long time, enchanted, unable to decide on which of its two banks you would choose to live with a loved one, forgetting the rest of mankind … Valleys with pretty white houses surrounded by trees, hillsides yellow with vines or white with cherry blossom, ancient walls covered by burgeoning honeysuckle, rose gardens from which slender towers suddenly arise, everything speaks of the fertility of the soil and the great age of its monuments, arousing one's interest in the works of its industrious inhabitants."

Alfred de Vigny, *Cinq-Mars…*, 1826

2

THE HERITAGE

The first purpose of a château was to make war. The peaceful countryside of the Loire, famed for its fertility and mild climate, was at the very heart of the violent struggles which shaped France. It would be naïve to see the châteaux as mere ornaments and their warlike fortifications, however atrophied, as operatic backdrops. The fighting was as fierce here as anywhere else: the Loire valley was one of the theatres in which the Hundred Years War and the Wars of Religion were fought. To lords and vassal alike, defence was a necessity and insecurity was second nature.

Almost all the gracious châteaux of the Loire are the hybrid offspring of fortresses with massive keeps and rows of machicolations. Fortresses remained the dominant model up to the building of Chambord (begun 1519), and feudal society, based on military power, remained the model for the class then rising, whose power was based on money. The newly enriched merchants had to adopt the costumes, privileges, titles and estates of the warlords, and the style of their châteaux too. The new lords were obliged to defend themselves: to ensure their own longevity, they had to ensure that of their châteaux too, and they continued to follow the model of the fortified castle as long as they could. Men enriched by commerce and the court had no status of their own; they were bound to the king, and took care to establish their claim to the only recognized bonds between vassal and sovereign, those symbolically conveyed by possession of a château. Consequently, they began by imitating the châteaux of knights who had feudal tenure and powers of jurisdiction. Architectural style followed in the footsteps of the gradually changing composition of the ruling class. The king alone was not obliged to follow the pattern and could introduce innovations.

The struggle for control of the desirable countryside of the Loire reached a climax around the year 1000, when Eudes and Foulques, the lords of Blois and Anjou, were fighting for Touraine. The latter consolidated his conquests by building the first stone keeps in the region, at first Langeais, then Loches, Montbazon and Montrichard. The earlier châteaux of the Loire had been wooden defensive structures; stone was introduced as a building material during the eleventh century. The first of these new châteaux were square, primitive buildings with no windows apart from loopholes, and no door except for an opening high in the wall, reached by a ladder that could be pulled up when the alarm was raised.

These were the distant ancestors of the châteaux of the Loire. Their ruins, standing on mottes, can still be seen, preserved out of respect rather than by chance. They were closely related to the châteaux of the Hundred Years War, the period when the Dauphin Charles, driven out of Paris by the civil war in June 1418, took refuge in his own territory of Touraine, where the loyal people of Tours and his strong fortress at Chinon could still provide him with a kingdom. Even here, the Burgundians had attacked, capturing Tours in 1417. On its way from Tours to Chinon, his court took the old Grandmont road, passing Turpenay and Rivarennes, and had to cross the Indre by the ford of Port-Huault at Cheillé. In April 1429, Joan of Arc took the same route in the other direction on her way from Chinon to Tours.

After crossing the river Charles came to the town of Azay-sur-l'Indre, which was still in his enemies' hands. He was obliged to fight, and on gaining the victory he burned the town and its castle and had the 354 defeated soldiers hanged from the battlements. Thereupon "the inhabitants left the said place and went to live elsewhere, and the said place remains almost uninhabited …".[10]

In 1442, by now King Charles VII, he was asked to authorize "the fortification and securing of the said place, Azay, with walls, towers, turrets, barbicans, watch towers, drawbridges, ditches, palings, and whatever other fortifications and entrenchments may be necessary for the said fortification, for the security, guarding and defence of the said town of Azay and the said petitioners …".[11]

In 1418 Charles retreated to Bourges. He was not beaten yet. The merchants had made common cause with the Anglo-Burgundians and driven him out of Paris, but he was still powerful. His darkest hour came five years later, with his defeat and withdrawal. The tide turned in the 1430s. He retook Paris in 1436, but the capital was not reconciled to the King, and he continued to govern it from a distance.

In Bourges, he created a court the equal of any other of the time, and, with it, a remarkable administrative system. He was protected here by his own lands and those of his allies: the rich Angevins, Kings of Naples and Provence, and the very wealthy duc de Bretagne, men whose power was consolidated by local industry and coastal trade. When Bourges itself was threatened by the Burgundians, however, Charles faced defeat. His only possible refuge was in the old fortresses of Touraine where he had sometimes stayed: Chinon, Amboise and Les Roches-Tranchelion. He barricaded himself in, but none of those châteaux was equipped to accommodate a court and a well-developed administration requiring rooms and offices, so he turned to the loyal and prosperous city of Tours, which could provide money and administrative officers, and installed his court at "Les Montils", now Plessis-lès-Tours, Louis XI's favourite residence. Charles VII was at the manor of Les Montils in 1444 when he received the English ambassadors who negotiated the end of the Hundred Years War. It took a further century for that war to fade from people's minds.

Another kind of architecture was beginning to develop alongside the fortified castles, literally in their shadow: a costlier and more delicate style of architecture. Courts were becoming richer and more dispersed as they grew. Within the ramparts of Nantes, the capital of the dukes of Brittany, one can still see an elegant staircase with narrow, timid bay-windows that serves the main building. There was a similar layout at Châteaudun, the home of Jean de Dunois, and at Angers, the residence of René d'Anjou, titular King of Sicily and Comte de Provence. To complete the metamorphosis, the ramparts had to be shed like a cast-off skin. At the "royal residences" of Amboise and Loches, the large, simple dwelling houses contrast with the fortifications, resting against them or rising above them, out of reach. Miniatures of the duc de Berry's proud châteaux of Saumur and Mehun-sur-Yèvre show the upper galleries ornately adorned with windows, metalwork and terraces. Chambord still reflects the style of these lofty buildings, where luxury flowered at the tops of inaccessible towers, but here apartments built for pleasure crown towers of moderate height, and there is not a battlement to be seen. The first châteaux of the Loire can thus be described as modifications to the former princely castles, made when princes grew rich. However, their history was only just beginning, for the new political situation in the kingdom soon led to a reorganization of courts, offices and power. These changes were directly reflected in the architecture against which this drama was played out.

Their military ancestors bequeathed to the châteaux of the Loire strategic sites and immediate surroundings consisting of steep slopes a moat, or an encircling river. The present château of Azay-le-Rideau is situated not where the old fortified castle once stood, but on the site of a manor house which was built on an island liable to flooding, and thus had a natural moat in the river

Pol de Limbourg
Les Très Riches Heures du Duc de Berry, c. 1415
The Temptation of Christ
View of the Château de Mehun-sur-Yèvre

Indre, whose course was dammed by mills. The deep, muddy reaches of the Indre are interspersed with subsidiary channels full of rushes and reeds, while the main waterway, with a fall almost twice as steep as the fall of the Loire, can become almost a torrent. In flat country, wide moats were long regarded as the most elementary form of defence. They were sometimes widened to the full length of a cannon-shot, becoming mirrors rather than moats; Plessis-Bourré and the later Villegongis illustrate this. Much later, the area of water around Azay-le-Rideau was created simply for the pleasure of the eye.

The legacy of the past may often be disguised, but we should not be deceived. The great lords of the early sixteenth century, whether military commanders or financiers, still needed fortifications, though for reasons different from those of their forebears. The period of peace at home, under

Château de Mehun-sur-Yèvre
1367–1390 for Jean de Berry
View from the old moat

the rule of Louis XII and François I (1494–1547), might suggest that the châteaux could now have dispensed with their defences. But fortifications were still built, though in an atrophied form; demand for them remained long after the feudal context had waned. It came from the new courtiers, office-holders and financiers who were busy renovating old manor houses. They had two reasons, one symbolic and the other practical.

The symbolic significance of fortifications was as valid as ever: control of the land and authority over its inhabitants still went with the manor and its tower, drawbridge and moat. The owner of the château was responsible for administering justice in the locality. The château itself was not so much a building as the fount of feudal authority. Its owner ruled an entire territory, "as the soul resides and exercises its force in all parts of the body", wrote the jurist Charles Loyseau in his *Traité des Seigneuries*.[12] The financial office-holders who aspired to the nobility were particularly anxious to preserve these symbols as a necessary confirmation of their power in the eyes of those from whom they had to levy taxes. The *nouveaux riches* are often ostentatious, and the newly ennobled, or candidates for ennoblement, were especially attached to the outward forms of feudal architecture, however unnecessary they might seem. The banker Bernard Salviati, father of Ronsard's Cassandre, whose business was at court in the city of Blois, owned the old château of Talcy nearby. He renovated it by adding a rather modern interior gallery in the Italian style, but when he came to the exterior he sought permission, around 1520, to fortify it with "walls, towers, battlements, barbicans, loopholes, machicolations, drawbridges, ramparts and other such defences serviceable to a fortified house …".[13] His petition was granted, but on condition that "he may not, by virtue of the said fortifications, in any manner whatsoever call himself a lord castellan, nor have the right of watch and ward …".

The idea of the château meant more to these men than the château itself, and to match that ideal, any new building had to imitate the prevailing model. In fact those who were most powerful took the least trouble to follow the pattern: in his great château of Bury near Blois, now destroyed, Florimond Robertet ventured, like the king himself, to make a gallery out of an entrance wing of the basic quadrilateral design. The château was flanked by strong but now purely symbolic towers, as Chambord would be.

However, it was primarily for reasons of security that features of the fortified castle persisted. The countryside was not safe, and while fortifications might seem archaic in the age of artillery, they were still an adequate means of defence against bands of brigands. Gilles Berthelot, the new lord of

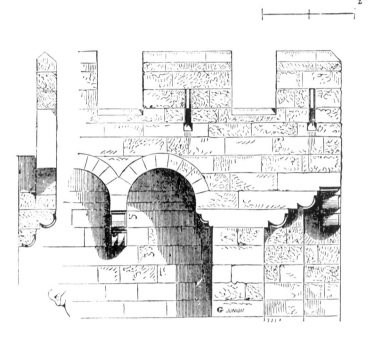

Azay-le-Rideau, asked the king to authorize the fortification of the town and chapel of Azay against "wicked rogues, notorious thieves and robbers lying in wait on the highway …".[14] There was good reason for these precautions: on 8 January 1515 marauding bands struck terror into Azay-le-Rideau when they mounted an attack, although the inhabitants managed to repel it.[15] It was prudent for for the château symbolizing its owner's legitimate authority to be a stronghold for his own safety too, for these financiers were not idle bureaucrats. Royal power was delegated to them, and they were responsible for levying the taxes from which they derived their own fortunes. They could resort to violence and might be violently opposed in return. They were hated, and rebellion was not uncommon. The goods they seized in their forays looked for all the world like loot, so it was hardly surprising if they fortified their châteaux to keep it safe. Later, in the second half of the sixteenth century, the old fortifications came back into service during the Wars of Religion, and those who had maintained them reaped the benefit. Théodore de Bèze tells us how, on 8 July 1561, a large body of six to seven hundred "fanatics" fell upon the town of Azay, where some thirty people had taken refuge in the Protestant church.[16] Massacres and looting were common all over Touraine until April 1568.

The most important of the socially significant and distinctive features of a château was undoubtedly the donjon or keep: the great tower. The fief depended on it, the system of jurisdiction went with it, and it was proudly conserved even when its defensive function had almost vanished. More a monument than a tower, it symbolized domination and surveillance, in which respect its only rival was the church-tower or belfry. When châteaux were modernized, their great towers were preserved. The tower at Châteaudun rises, isolated, in the middle of the courtyard, like a votive

E. Viollet-le-Duc
Dictionnaire raisonné de l'Architecture française …,
1854–1868
Machicolations of Royat church

column. At Chenonceaux the main part of the Bohier family's château is not attached to the keep either, but the tower was piously maintained, standing alone like a symbolic vestige of the feudal order, the massive effect lightened by a set of ornamented windows. Usually, however, the new château incorporated the old tower, leaning on it as if to draw strength and significance from it. At Azay-le-Rideau the largest of the towers, the north tower flanking the corner of the château built at a much later date, is still, despite the anodyne 19th-century restoration, the original medieval structure from which the Renaissance château seems to have developed. The mason in charge of the Renaissance work seems to have had difficulty integrating the tower. He was obliged to build a diagonal wall to incorporate it into the new structure, thus showing how much store was set on its preservation. At Chaumont-sur-Loire, the Amboise tower above the river Loire still has the genuine look of a fortress in the wing that it dominates. It must have suited Diane de Poitiers; sent into exile here by Catherine de Medici, she had the old parapet walk restored and adorned with her coat of arms between 1560 and 1566, either as a gesture of defiance or perhaps for her own security.[17]

These military structures form the core of almost all the châteaux, even when they have been renovated and opened out so that their rugged outlines are no longer in evidence. The old ramparts of Blois, flanked by the Châtellerault tower to the west, were not demolished but entirely concealed beneath the magnificent façade of loggias in the Italian style built over them by François I and Queen Claude, and still form its backbone.

The châteaux of the Loire *are* fortified strongholds. The grace we admire in the terrace at Chaumont with its wide views of the Loire, or in the turrets of Ussé looking out over the valley of the Indre, is deceptive. In both cases it is the result of a later owner's demolition of a wing, on the most picturesque side, which once completed the sombre quadrilateral design: the north wing at Ussé was demolished in the seventeenth century and at Chaumont in the eighteenth century. If the walls of Azay-le-Rideau had been completed they would probably have been joined to the great tower on its north side, closing off the view available today from the attractive right-angled structure that was finally built.

The later châteaux of the Loire, however, esteemed comfort above security. The entrance wing has shrunk until it is only a gallery, a place to receive visitors rather than a fortification. The once dominating angle towers have been reduced to the size of four-square pavilions resembling houses.

Similarly at Chambord, the last of the great châteaux of the Loire, the roofs of the lateral towers are set directly on cornices, and no provision is made for the formerly indispensable parapet walk with its loopholes, battlements and machicolations. Yet this tradition was still observed by the architects of Azay-le-Rideau, L'Islette, and long afterwards by the builders of Le Lude, Valençay and even Villegongis.

One reason for this change was the changed situation of the French monarchy. After Louis XII, the king held undisputed sway over his vassals. Only the king could afford to demolish the great tower that dominated the château courtyard, as he did at Bourges and Blois, and finally at the Louvre, the national tower which was said to "control all the fiefs of the kingdom".[18]

The architectural conservatism of the feudal lords, wedded as they were to the powers and privileges reflected in the layout of their castles, was in strong contrast to the sense of liberation that developed in royal architecture at the very time when the contested and bellicose institution of suzerainty was being transformed into absolute monarchy. Between the two stood the growing power of finance, resulting from the enrichment of the kingdom and the boom in trade and money-lending. Certain prominent bourgeois were its beneficiaries. They still had no specific place in the social order, but their luxurious homes resembled those of the king whom they so loyally served, while retaining the outward appearance of the châteaux of the age of chivalry with which they still felt obliged to identify. The history of the châteaux of the Loire is the history of this political collusion.

E. Viollet-le-Duc
Dictionnaire raisonné de l'Architecture française ...,
1854–1868
Machicolations of King René's gate at Tarascon

ABOVE:
View of the town and Château de Chinon
Engraving, late 18th century

BELOW:
Château de Chinon
2nd half of the 10th century–15th century
for Thibaut le Tricheur, reinforced by
Henry II Plantagenet (King of England)
in the 12th century
Fortifications seen from the banks of the Vienne

Château de Châteaudun
1459–1532, built for Jean de Dunois, François I
and François II de Longueville
North view from the banks of the Loir

The inaccessible château

… The choice of a site was vital in military architecture, and the custom
of building on a hill or beside a river was maintained in the châteaux
of the Loire …

The defensive wall

… The first stone châteaux were built in the 11th century in Touraine, where the limestone was easily worked and wars were bitterly fought, giving rise to a particularly strong tradition of fortified castles …

Château de Loches
11th to second half of 14th century
Keep, 11th century, for Foulques Nerra
Views of exterior and interior

Above:
Château de Montrichard
begun 1120 for Hugues I d'Amboise
Enceinte and keep

ABOVE:
Château de Semblançay
Early 16th century, for Jacques de Beaune
de Semblançay
Enceinte and round towers

BELOW:
Château de Chinon
1205–1370, for Philippe Auguste
The Fort du Coudray, Tour du Moulin,
Tour de Boisy and Donjon du Coudray

Château de Loches
11th to second half of 16th century
Fortifications of the keep, 12th–13th century

The ramparts

… The ramparts surrounded the château, enclosing it within walls
and defensive towers, a pattern which still persisted at the time of
the first renaissance of the châteaux of the Loire …

The keep

… The keep or donjon had great symbolic value: the lord's right of jurisdiction depended on it. Even when it was of no further military use, it was long retained to assert the privileges of the nobility …

ABOVE:
Château de Chaumont
Tour d'Amboise
begun 1465 for Pierre d'Amboise

RIGHT:
Château de Châteaudun
Keep of Thibaut V, late 12th century

BELOW:
Château de Chenonceaux
Keep known as the "Tour des Marques"
begun 1432 for Jean II Marques

Château du Moulin
1490–1506, for Philippe du Moulin

Above:
View from the north: the fortress and
the main building
Right:
View from the east: the great tower

Facing Page:
Château du Plessis-Bourré
1468–1473, for Jean Bourré
View from the moat

Château de Chaumont
1498–1510, for Charles II d'Amboise
Entrance towers and drawbridge

<small>RIGHT AND FACING PAGE ABOVE:</small>
Drawbridge and piers
<small>ABOVE:</small>
View of the whole structure

Château de Châteaudun
1459–1532, for Jean de Dunois, François I
and François II de Longueville
Parapet walk

CENTRE:
Château de Chaumont
Entrance tower, 1498–1510
Machicolations with emblems of Diane
de Poitiers, restored c. 1560

RIGHT:
Château de Fougères-sur-Bièvre
1475–1520, for Pierre de Refuge
North-east tower, machicolations on corbels

FACING PAGE:
Château de Talcy
begun 1520, for Bernard Salviati
Square entrance tower: machicolations,
crenels and merlons

Parapet walks and machicolations

…With the end of the feudal wars, defensive features became purely decorative, but remained an essential part of the architecture of the château: the parapet wall became a cornice and the machicolations an ornamental crown …

3

THE NEW KINGS

"The best fortress in the world is the affection of the people", counselled Machiavelli in 1512 in *Il Principe* (The Prince). No princes of the period were in a better position to follow his advice than the kings of France. The Italianization of politics inevitably brought with it an Italianate style of architecture. To understand why the heavy curtain walls around the castle keeps came down so quickly in France, revealing façades of lace-like ornamentation, we need to grasp that, though the wars were over and prosperity (even opulence for some) had returned, these ostentatious palaces, built, unlike fortified castles, to dazzle rather than dismay, were nonetheless intended to awe commoner and foreigner alike. France waged war in Italy, but at home, in a country now united, she preferred the artifice of diplomacy, sometimes described as the continuation of war by other means. Louis XII and François I were therefore able to put the advice of their contemporary Machiavelli into practice; he had also written, "The matter may be summed up as follows: the prince who fears his own people more than he fears foreigners must build fortifications, but he who fears foreigners more must do the opposite".[19]

The struggle between baron and monarch was over. At its darkest hour, "the King of Bourges" (Charles VII) had been forced to abandon Bourges itself and take shelter in his Touraine fortresses, close to his last remaining allies, Anjou and Brittany. From this struggle, the kings of France had emerged victorious.

Louis XI, his son, patiently unified and pacified his kingdom. On René d'Anjou's death in 1480 he acquired Anjou, Maine and Provence; Picardy, Burgundy and the Franche-Comté reverted to the crown after the death in 1477 of Charles the Bold. The king's success in turning this desperate situation to his own advantage was neither miraculous nor due solely to his own abilities. Under attack from the last of the great feudal lords, Louis XI allied himself with the urban bourgeoisie, playing off city against château and commerce against chivalry.

Today, all that remains of his fortified château of Le Plessis-lès-Tours is the pleasant lodging of a bourgeois king: a plain, brick-built house surrounded by a simple garden. There is a striking similarity between this house and the Hôtel de la Petite Bourdaisière, built in Tours (a town whose growing prosperity the king encouraged) for one of those middle-class men whose loyalty he had won, and the resemblance between the two reflects a profound ideological sympathy between the rich urban bourgeoisie and the new royal power. This was a grave danger for the nobility. Their own ambition had exposed them to it, and it proved fatal to them. The great châteaux of the Loire were not, for the most part, the mansions of the aristocracy; they belonged to the officials who had replaced the nobility at the king's side.

None the less, Le Plessis-lès-Tours had formidable defences. The first bourgeois king's new home was fortified as long as he felt directly threatened, but the defences were architecturally separate from the main building, surrounding it without actually touching it, like a skin about to be shed. Buildings more attractive than their predecessors were already being constructed inside the walled bailey at Nantes, Châteaudun and Loches, and soon after at Amboise. A prince who feared no usurpers, such as King René, could venture to prefer a manor to a castle and an open garden to a fortified terrace. Although fortifications were still much in evidence, René d'Anjou, King of Provence and Naples, was probably the first to dispense with them, not so much in his châteaux at Angers – where the manor house still stood behind forbidding walls – or at Baugé, as in his country manors of Launay near Saumur and La Ménitré near Angers. When the king of France in his own turn had nothing and no one to fear, he too stripped his châteaux of their defences, but enhanced their splendour. It was not enough to feel confident; one had to *seem* confident too.

Under the regency of the Beaujeus, while Louis XI's son (the future Charles VIII) was a minor, final tremors of unrest gave the great feudal lords some hope of shaking off the power closing in on them. This was the Mad War *(Guerre folle)*, or first "Fronde", and the revolt showed the nobility as a class in decline and disarray. It was led by the king's cousin, Louis d'Orléans, and once he inherited the crown on the death of Charles VIII and became King Louis XII (1498), the last of the feudal opposition could be said to have been rendered impotent. The age of the absolute monarchy had come, and it was to last until the eighteenth century.

Aristocratic warlords were of no great value in peacetime. Their diminishing power was frittered away in useless rebellions. The recovery of the kingdom was the work of a new force, founded on labour and financial exchange. Under Louis XII France was no longer just a kingdom but a powerful and highly regarded nation state. Its king was respected as master of his domains; he reigned over a good administration, a reasonably equitable juridical system, and an excellent army, particularly strong in artillery. The end of the wars, a gradual process which had begun in the mid-fifteenth century, signalled a major economic revival; it facilitated trade with modern countries equipped with more modern methods of production – Flanders, the Rhine valley, northern Italy – in fact, the advent of commerce on a grand scale. The discovery of the New World augmented the influx of money; this was a period when prices rose and fortunes were made. The cities in particular profited by this new prosperity, and took pride in it, but there was a drawback: the heavy burden of taxation, which Louis XI had justified by citing the necessities of war. Louis XII, inheriting a booming economy in a period of peace at home, was actually able to reduce taxes, a thing unheard of in centuries past, which earned him the name of "Father of the people" and his reign the reputation of a Golden Age.

The city of Blois resembled a huge building-site; every courtier, banker and merchant was erecting his own private house. There is a family likeness between the gallery Louis XII built at the entrance to his château in 1504, and its counterpart built by his principal financier Florimond Robertet for his mansion in the city centre, the Hôtel d'Alluye. But while great watch- towers still flanked a perfect quadrilateral at the vast Château de Bury two leagues outside Blois, also built by Robertet, and the gallery leading into the château had entrance towers on both sides, all the towers had gone from the royal Château de Blois. On at least three sides, open galleries with broad balconies delimited the courtyard area, offering no protection from the town, and the entry to the château formed part of the bailey. The king must have ordered the demolition of the keep repaired by his father, Charles d'Orléans, before erecting these buildings. The first true metamorphosis of the châteaux of the Loire, then, took place at Blois between 1498 and 1504.

As in Italy, the new balance of social power made itself felt; bourgeois democracy emerged. For the time being at least, it was in harmony with absolute monarchy, for the king protected the townspeople and relied on the new force they represented. In 1484, before the *Guerre folle*, the Estates General met at Tours, and the third estate obtained very extensive privileges: the right to be consulted before any tax was levied, and the admission of its delegates even to the king's own Council.

Louis XII, a man of forthright and sometimes headstrong character, was

Royal emblem
Porcupine of Louis XII
Château de Blois, Louis XII wing

advised for better or worse by his wife, Anne de Bretagne, and by Cardinal Georges d'Amboise. He played the part of a moderate, enlightened, absolute monarch, on the model formulated in Italy in Machiavelli's *Il Principe*, and in France by the king's supporters Claude de Seyssel, in *La Grande Monarchie de France*, and Charles de Grassaille, in his *Regalium Franciae*.[20] At the same period, this new, all-conquering concept of royalty gave birth to an idea from which the destiny of the kings of France was never again free: the theory of regicide.

The king was on display in his châteaux, undefended. Foreign ambassadors and princes, men who could or would be his enemies, were welcomed by Louis XII with great ceremony to the renovated Château de Blois. Archduke Philip of Austria, the king's adversary in every respect and a man from whom he had much to fear, was invited to Blois, and received there not with armed force but with festivities. The people were much moved. Erasmus congratulated the king. It was not so long since Louis XI had gone to Péronne at the invitation of Charles the Bold to conduct negotiations and been taken prisoner, or since Archduke Philip himself, shipwrecked on the shores of England, had been captured by order of Henry VIII. However, the new policies set out in *Il Principe* were at work. On the way from Flanders to Spain, Archduke Philip came to Blois on 8 December 1501; a retinue of dignitaries had attended him all the way from Orléans and followed in his train to the gates of Blois, where cardinals and princes met him for a triumphal entry into the city.[21] A household consisting of a hundred servants and four hundred archers was placed at his disposal. That evening he entered the château between a double line of archers and Swiss guards, each with a halberd in one hand and a torch in the other (it was December), "so that it was bright as day". This was the purpose of the new style of château: the archduke was received first in the great hall, hung with tapestries depicting the Trojan War, and then in the banqueting hall, hung arrayed with cloth of gold, where pavilions of green damask had been erected. A number of camp beds draped with green, red or black damask had been set up in the bedchamber, for the most important members of the archduke's retinue; he himself had a bed with a canopy of cloth of gold lined with white damask, and curtains of red and yellow taffeta. He slept in fine cambric sheets, beneath four-branched silver chandeliers hanging from silver chains, and had the use of a sideboard, a gilded chair "very well made and worked, brought from Italy", and two or three "wardrobes" to which no one else had access. A sombre château of the old style would have made a poor setting for these new functions.

Architecture had to open out and become more ornamental; at this early stage of the Renaissance period – from the reign of Louis XII to the beginning of the reign of François I – it owed more to Machiavelli than Bramante. The new château was devised for armies of a new kind: armies of courtiers, officials and pages. The king's court evolved in the image of those of the most magnificent princes of the day, emulating the luxury and ceremonial of the court of the dukes of Burgundy, who had founded a new courtly civilization. Louis XII had 322 people in his private service.[22] The "king's household" comprised 2 chamberlains, 13 *maîtres d'hôtel*, 7 pantlers, 7 cup-bearers, 6 carvers (of meat), 13 squires, 30 "children of honour", 22 valets, 11 butlers, 10 ushers, 1 secretary, 3 sergeants-at-arms, 18 heralds and 33 clerks. The royal kitchen employed 5 squires, 7 pantlers, 8 cup-bearers, and 11 chefs to cook the finer dishes, while the lower kitchen staff consisted of 4 squires, 10 butlers, 16 cup-bearers, 18 chefs, 8 soup-makers, 8 fruiterers, 4 sauce-makers and 7 errand boys and scullions. Besides these 256 servants with their more or less honorific titles, there was a troop of 66 pages. Every courtier and great functionary who was close to the king had his own "household", and according to Brantôme it was Queen Anne who set up the first *cour de Dames*, the "Court of Ladies".[23]

All this meant that a great many people had to be accommodated in the château. In fact only the king, the queen and a few very elevated personages had a bed, a rare and impressive piece of furniture. The rest slept on straw mattresses anywhere they could. The great halls were all state apartments,

Royal emblem
Salamander of François I
Château de Chambord, the keep,
Guardroom

with their furnishings reduced to a minimum, basically consisting of chests, and planks laid over trestles and covered with cloths, easily dismantled and removed. On the other hand, tapestries were hung everywhere as soon as the king arrived. At Amboise, 4,000 hooks were needed to hang the tapestries when Anne de Bretagne came on a visit, and the largest body of workers in the château consisted of the *liciers* whose job it was to put them up. For the court was itinerant, and most of the time the châteaux stood empty, so it is not surprising to find them empty today (or else, alas, furnished with mediocre pieces from much later periods). The king wrote on a plank resting on two trestles, and slept in a plain camp bed.

The castle population was more than the bailey and its surroundings could accomodate. The military guard which accompanied the king consisted of 100 *lances* (men-at-arms and their followers), amounting to nearly 500 men in his personal guard, while the rest of the train comprised 1,180 *lances* (some 5,000 soldiers). Then there were the "itinerant merchants following the court", who supplied all its provisions, not to mention unauthorized hangers-on and prostitutes. These people were not accommodated in the château, but camped outside it. The "venery of tents", consisting of a hundred archers and fifty carts, each drawn by six horses, drove the tents around the country and put them up wherever the king went.[24] This great royal circus even had its menagerie: the stable was the most expensive of the royal services, and the king poured more money into it than he spent on building his châteaux. There were hundreds of ordinary hounds, and Louis XII kept nine dozen greyhounds in addition. Falconry, too, was important. The king's aviaries at Le Plessis-lès-Tours and Blois were famous, competing with each other in keeping rare species, herons and parrots. The Italian princes had exported the fashion for keeping wild animals; in Milan, they used leopards to course hares. King René was proud of his lions. Hunting was far more than a pastime; for a long period, it was a consuming passion. Louis XII was once seen to abandon a procession in pursuit of game, and we are told that François I himself marked out the boundaries of the park at Chambord.

It is impossible to imagine a château without its surrounding gardens and forest. Chambord was built as a hunting lodge. At Blois, you could leave the buildings of the château and go along the *galerie des Cerfs* (Stags' Gallery) to the huge gardens, known to us now only from Du Cerceau's engravings, and thence on into the forest.

The court, swollen with functionaries and servants, spilled over into the town. The greatest dignitaries, such as the Cardinal d'Amboise, who was the king's first minister, and Dinteville, Master of the Royal Hunt, had their own houses in the bailey of the Château de Blois. Meanwhile, stone replaced timber for the building of houses to accommodate bankers and artists in the still mediaeval streets of the old town. Pacello da Mercogliano, designer of the great gardens, lived in the suburb of Vienne, perhaps to be near his nurseries, and Jacques Sourdeau, the master mason, lived in the suburb of Le Foix below the castle, while the architect Dominique de Cortone lived in the town itself. So did the painters Bouteloup and Etienne de la Salle, the glaziers, tapestry-makers, tailors, enamellers, cutlers, goldsmiths and clockmakers. The king's services and their staff also invaded the town: the chancery had to be accommodated, the stables with all their grooms and farriers, the arsenal, the storehouses for salt, grain and fodder. Besides the civil and military members of the household there was the religious staff attached to any great family: at Blois, for example, it included the canons of St-Calais, the chapel of the château, and of the collegiate church of St-Sauveur in the bailey. Under Louis XII the churches of St-Martin and St-Honoré in the town of Blois were rebuilt. Queen Claude began the rebuilding of St-Solenne, later to be the cathedral. The royal accounts contain intriguing little passages illustrating the diverse and sometimes unexpected nature of the court's requirements. Louis XII bought a room in the town for the clockmakers whom he had commissioned to make him a copper sphere, and rented another room in which to store the cheeses, "five years old", that the maréchal de Gié had brought

Royal emblem
Ermine of Claude of France
Château d'Azay-le-Rideau
North front, the great staircase
Window base

him back from Milan. It is easy to picture the hurry and bustle in Blois when the court came to town, and the permanent wealth it derived from such visits.[25]

The empty, echoing château, where further building work was always in progress, was only a staging post for the court, which spent more time on the roads of the Loire valley than in its châteaux. Each of them assumed its own function in the increasingly dense network. The king governed from Blois, especially in the winter months.

He went to deal with his affairs in Paris, where he lodged at the Tournelles, and then in Lyon, travelling up the Loire as far as Roanne. From Lyon, he went on to the wars in Italy. It took the court a month to reach Italy, although a courier coming from Venice needed only twelve days to make the journey in the other direction. On his way, the king went hunting at Montfrault near Chambord, which was already famous for its game, and saw his councillors, visiting Georges d'Amboise at the Château de Chaumont-sur-Loire and Florimond Robertet at the Château de Bury. The royal Château d'Amboise, garrisoned by men under the command of the maréchal de Gié, was still maintained as a stronghold in a now rather old-fashioned style. The young Comte d'Angoulême, who succeeded Louis XII as François I in 1515, spent his childhood there before he married his cousin Claude, the king's daughter. Amboise is easily reached along the Loire. Close to Blois, whose defences had now come down, it preserved the appearance of a fortified castle. Its usefulness was shown at the time of the famous 1560 *conjuration*, when the court, fearing that the Huguenot conspirators would take Blois by surprise, beat a hasty retreat to Amboise, where the attack was quickly repulsed.

Louis XII also stayed at Le Plessis-lès-Tours, where he held council, and at Montrichard on the Cher, which he had only recently acquired, to celebrate the betrothal of Claude de France and François. His officials stayed not far away in the châteaux of Beauregard, Fougères-sur-Bièvre, Herbault-en-Sologne and Cheverny; the last-named had been bought by his master of artillery. These châteaux of the Loire may thus be regarded as a cluster of residences in which the court assembled to be near the absolute monarch, as it gradually beame part and parcel of the monarch's centralised power.

The château cannot be understood in isolation from these courtly satellites which drew the new political map of the kingdom, or without the indispensable jousting lists, gardens and forests that surrounded it. Chambord, the last of the royal châteaux of the Loire, was a park before it was a château. The impulsive, young King François I created around 1519 it as a last, imposing piece of chivalric scenery, anachronistic even at the time of its building; and that is certainly how his contemporaries saw it. No one actually lived in it; it was not a residence but a symbol. The court of François I spent only a few days there during his forty-year reign; it was not a seat of government like Le Plessis-lès-Tours, Amboise or Blois.

Nor was it a fortress like Loches or Chinon: its towers had no loopholes and its terraces no battlements. Its strength was its imposing charm; it was the stone-built equivalent of the Field of the Cloth of Gold, and the Holy Roman Emperor, Charles V, François's rival for the imperial crown, was invited to come and marvel at it. One might almost suspect the king of building it solely for Charles's visit. It was a place for hunting, festivities and lavish processions, its terraces designed for watching those activities: it was built for the staging of spectacles, and the real spectacle to be admired was the display of royal power. It still preserved a basic allusion to the military château, with its quadrilateral layout flanked by strong towers, but the fortress-like parts were kept low, and the buildings then rose to a delicate keep and were crowned by lace-like ornamental architecture and a lantern. An amazing staircase stood in the middle of this notional fortress. It was almost certainly the brainchild of Leonardo da Vinci,[26] who had devised still more complicated designs. It occupied almost the whole of the central area, clearly identifying the Château de Chambord not as a residence, still less as a residence, but as a votive monument to the absolute monarchy, a quasi-mystical ascension to centralized power, a temple to the new kings.

The manors of René d'Anjou

"… He came to see your castle, where he found Monsieur your son, accompanied by your servants, Monsieur de Précigny being absent with the king, where he still remains. He saw your gardens and pavilion and your lions, and he seemed wonderfully content with everything. The said duke went to La Ménitré, where he supped, slept and dined, which no-one had any idea he would till very early on the day he set off. Furnishings were brought at once from Beaufort to appoint the place as well as might be, although for so short a time, and in such a manner that the duke was marvellously well pleased. They gave him some of your calves, which were eaten there and then. They were young and fat, and the duke said that he had never in his life eaten anything nearly so good. As yet we do not know whether he went to Launay or not."

Account of a visit of the duc de Bretagne to King René

LEFT:
René d'Anjou
Mortifiement de Vaine Plaisance, c. 1458
The King in his Study…

René d'Anjou
Mortifiement de Vaine Plaisance, c. 1458

LEFT:
The Coachman driving the Queen …
ABOVE:
Woman about to cross the Bridge …

Manor of King René d'Anjou

FACING PAGE ABOVE:
Manoir de Baugé, begun 1455
BELOW:
Manoir de Launay, pre-1480

ABOVE:
Château du Plessis-lès-Tours
After 1474–1505, originally for Louis XI
East wing, main building

FACING PAGE ABOVE AND BELOW:
Tours (Indre-et-Loire)
Hôtel de la Petite Bourdaisière
Late 15th century, built for the Babou de la
Bourdaisière family
Main building and first-floor window

Royal architecture and bourgeois architecture

"… First, hardly anyone entered Plessis du Parc lez Tours (where he was residing) except for the domestic servants and archers, of whom he had four hundred, a good number of them keeping watch every day, patrolling the place and guarding the gate. No lord nor any great personage lodged there, and scarcely any company of great lords came in. Indeed, none went there but Monseigneur de Beaujeu, now Duke of Bourbon, the king's son-in-law. And he had a great grid of iron bars built all around the said Plessis, with iron spikes having several points fixed into the wall and at the entrance, where there was access to the moat. He also had four bastions made of iron, very thick, in places where a man could draw a bow at his ease, and that was a very splendid work costing over twenty thousand francs. Finally he stationed forty cross-bowmen by the moat night and day, with orders to draw a bow on any man who came near the place at night, until such time as the gate was opened in the morning."

Philippe de Commynes, *Mémoires*, Book VI, 1498

The royal châteaux: Loches

"… The king and queen took leave of Lyon with all their retinue, and set out to return to France, and they travelled so far that around Martinmas they reached Loches, where their daughter Madame Claude was, and they stayed there until after the feast of Christmas. During that time the king held his Estates at Loches, and sent out the envoys who were then at court. And the Cardinal d'Amboise also began to exercise the office of his legation, which he had not done during the journey from beyond the Alps."

Jean d'Auton, *Chroniques*, 1502

Château de Loches, the royal residence
Old Lodge, late 14th century,
residence of Charles VII
New Lodge, late 15th to early 16th century,
for Charles VIII and Louis XII

Facing Page:
Old Lodge and New Lodge
Above:
Interior courtyard in front of the royal
apartments
Left:
Old Lodge and the Agnès Sorel Tower

Amboise

"... Charles the eighth of that name was in his château of Amboise, where he had put in hand the greatest building works that ever a king began in a hundred years, both in the château and the town, as may be seen in the towers to which one ascends on horseback and in the works undertaken in the town to plans laid out with wonderful effort and expense, and the work was not yet nearly finished. Moreover, he brought many excellent artisans from Naples, masters of various crafts, such as carvers of stone and painters, and his works seemed to be the undertaking of a young king who had no thought of death but hoped for a long life, for he brought together all the fair things he had been shown to rejoice him, in whatever country, whether it were France, Italy or Flanders, and his heart was always set on returning to Italy."

Philippe de Commynes, *Mémoires,* Book VIII, 1498

Château d'Amboise
Reversion of the seigneurie of Amboise to
the crown, 1431
Reconstruction of the château, 1492–post-1515

FACING PAGE ABOVE:
View from the banks of the Loire
FACING PAGE BELOW:
Royal apartments, Charles VIII wing,
1492–1498
ABOVE:
The terrace, gardens originallly designed
by Pacello da Mercogliano
RIGHT:
Royal apartments and gallery joining them
to the "apartments of the royal children"
(now destroyed)

Château de Blois
Château of the counts of Blois, a royal
residence from 1498
Louis XII wing, 1498–1504

Left and Below:
Gargoyle on the cornice of the forecourt
façade
Facing Page:
Entrance with equestrian statue of Louis XII
(copy dating from 1857)

Above:
Jean Marot
Le Voyage de Gênes, 1507
The entry of Louis XII into Genoa

Louis XII at Blois

"… The feast of Christmas being over, the king left Loches and went
to his château of Blois, which he made all new, and so magnificent
that it seemed a royal work indeed, and there he stayed until the end
of the month of February with the queen and his daughter Madame
Claude."

Jean d'Auton, *Chroniques*, 1502

Architecture opening up to new policies

"… saying first that the very Christian King Louis, twelfth of that name, was in his city of Blois at the beginning of the said year one thousand five hundred and six, and the queen with him and their daughter Madame Claude, who was seven or eight years old, very beautiful and very well educated: and there they passed the time in great joy and pleasure, for the king was very healthy and in good spirits, and all his country was happy and at peace, with wealth abounding. It happened that at that time, at the end of the month of April, mindful of affairs of state the king went to Tours, and the queen and Madame Claude with him."

Jean d'Auton, *Chroniques,* 1506

Château de Blois
Louis XII wing, 1498–1504

FACING PAGE:
View of the state courtyard
LEFT AND BELOW:
Louis XII gallery: window, arcades,
and foot of the state staircase

Transitional areas

Château d'Amboise
Royal apartments, Charles VIII wing,
1492–1498,
and Tour des Minimes, 1495–1498

RIGHT:
Ramp inside the Tour des Minimes
BELOW:
Access to the château terrace

Château d'Amboise
Royal apartments, Charles VIII wing,
1492–1498,
and Tour des Minimes, 1495–1498

ABOVE:
Covered gallery looking out on the Loire

The austere "residence"
of an itinerant court

Château de Fougères-sur-Bièvre
1475–1520, for Pierre de Refuge
Guardroom

FACING PAGE ABOVE RIGHT:
P. Bernard de Montfaucon
Les Monumens de la monarchie française
Louis XII surrounded by his lords
Paris, 1729–1733

Château de Châteaudun
Dunois wing, 1459–1469

FACING PAGE ABOVE LEFT AND BELOW:
Great hall and window embrasure
LEFT:
Kitchen

The queen's household

"... So all flocked to her, and few came away unsatisfied. Above all, she was famous for cherishing her domestic servants and doing much good to them. She it was who first set up the great Court of Ladies, which has lasted from her time until this day; for she had a very large retinue of both ladies and girls, and never refused to admit any, on the contrary she would ever enquire of the gentlemen at court, their fathers, whether they had daughters and of what condition they were, and then she would ask those gentlemen to send her the girls."

Brantôme (c. 1540–1614), *Vie des Dames illustres, discours sur la Reyne Anne de Bretagne...*

ABOVE:
Blois (Loir-et-Cher)
Pavilion of Anne de Bretagne, 1499–1514
The queen's monogram

LEFT:
Jean Marot
Le Voyage de Gênes, 1507
The Book given by its Author to Queen Anne de Bretagne

RIGHT:
The Story of David and Bathsheba,
c. 1510–1515
Queen Michol and the lords on the balcony
Tapestry
Musée de la Renaissance, Ecouen

RIGHT:
Château d'Amboise
Chapelle St-Hubert, 1492–1496
Vault of the chapel

From austerity to magnificence

Château de Blois
François I wing, 1515–pre-1524
Hall on the first floor

Facing Page Below:
Tympanum of doorway
Above:
Ornamental mantelpiece with the royal
emblem

Château de Villandry
Kitchen garden, laid out for Jean Le Breton,
from 1536

AMBOYSE

LE PLAN DE TOVT LE LIEV
PLANVM TOTIVS LOCI

Jacques Androuet du Cerceau
Les plus Excellents Bastiments de France,
1576–1579
Château d'Amboise

The gardens

"… Dear brother, I must tell you that it was not enough for me to have had my face marred with the smallpox, but I have also had the measles, of which, thank God, I am cured. Furthermore, you would not believe how beautiful are the gardens I have in this town, for upon my faith, it seems that they lack only Adam and Eve to make them an earthly Paradise, they are so fair and full of all fine and remarkable things, as I hope to tell you, but when I see you. I have also found the best of painters in this country, and I will send you some of them to make the most beautiful ceilings imaginable. In point of beauty and richness, the ceilings in Beauce, Lyon and other parts of France in no way approach those to be seen here, so I mean to provide myself with such painters and bring them back to do the same at Amboise."

Charles VIII, *Lettres de Naples*, 28 March 1495

ABOVE AND FACING PAGE:
Château de Blois
François I wing, 1515–pre-1524
Staircase, ornamentation of the base,
1519–1520

RIGHT:
Château de Blois
Terrace with fountain, early 16th century,
formerly in the château gardens

Decoration in the Italian style

"… Blois is a fair city, situated in a pleasant place on the right bank of the Loire, adorned with fine houses, and densely populated. Its palace, which is very handsome, was built partly by Louis XII and partly by the reigning king. There you can admire two pretty gardens, one of them having a maze with a wooden fence around it and a terrace in the middle, also made of wood. At the entrance to the garden you may see two great stag's antlers, sent to King Louis from Germany as a wonderful curiosity."

Andrea Navagero, *Voyage d'André Navagero en Espagne et en France,* 1528

Château de Chambord
Begun 1519, for François I

ABOVE:
View of the château and the Cosson canal
FACING PAGE:
Terrace of the keep, 1519–1539

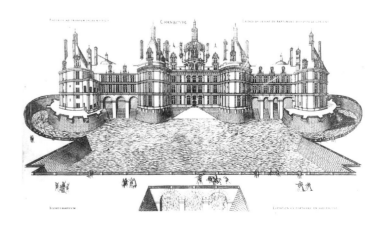

RIGHT:
Jacques Androuet du Cerceau,
Les plus Excellents Bastiments de France,
1576–1579
Chambord, south-east façade

Chambord, a château built to charm and inspire awe

"...What is to be said of Chambord, which incomplete as it is, only half finished, casts everyone who sees it into wonder and admiration? Why, that if the work could have been accomplished according to the plans it might be ranked among the wonders of the world, for that great and overweening king even wished to divert an arm of the river Loire past the walls (or as some say, the whole river), changing its course and turning its destination to his own ends..."

Brantôme (c. 1540–1614), *Vie des Hommes illustres, ...*

4
THE NEW LORDS

Azay-le-Rideau, Chenonceaux and other châteaux no longer extant, like
Bury are often connected in people's minds with the royal châteaux, this
at least partly because the men who built them were scarcely less wealthy
than the king. And their wealth was to a large extent involved with his. The
Renaissance was not the work of a single prince. It was the product of great
fortunes and the new economy then developing, one that did not depend
solely on the possession of land, but on money lending and the production
and free circulation of goods. The builders of the new palaces were not
warriors but financiers: they included Jacques de Beaune at Semblançay,
Florimond Robertet at Bury, Thomas Bohier at Chenonceaux, Gilles Berthelot at Azay-le-Rideau, the Alamands at Le Gué-Péan, and many other less
famous names.

The unsophisticated organization of the royal finances gave these men
enormous power. The merchant who provided the king and his large court
with all their needs was also the *contrôleur* (controller) of his expenses: Jacques
Coeur combined both functions, very much to his own advantage. This
merchant administering his client's income, was also the man who levied
the taxes from which that principally derived. These were the functions accumulated by the great office-holders, who were simultaneously tradesmen,
bankers, tax collectors and ministers. Such a system naturally fostered corrup-
tion, venality and nepotism, and legal action taken by the king to counter
abuses often became hopelessly entangled in complexities. When Charles VII
had regained power between 1436 and 1450, he set in train a remarkable and
durable reorganization of the financial administration. In the four fiscal
areas into which France was divided, it distinguished between officials who
supervised the finances (*the généraux des finances*, administering the king's
"extraordinary" revenues; the *trésoriers*, administering the king's "ordinary"
revenues; and the *contrôleurs*), and those who handled them (the *receveurs*
and *changeurs*). The men who held these appointments often accumulated
several positions, if not personally then at least within the family. They made
fortunes, particularly when the financial recovery of the kingdom, which had
begun around 1450, became firmly established during the second half of the
century. And, of course, these manipulators of money, purveyors and controllers of the royal finances, were fully acquainted with the murkiest affairs
of state.

When Charles VII went to reside in Bourges he had to set up his "household" there. It was to be a court worthy of the magnificent princes with whom
he must compete: the rulers of Burgundy, Anjou, Brittany and even the princes
of Italy. The merchants of Bourges provided him with cloth, weapons and
livestock. Pierre Coeur was the cleverest and most highly regarded of these
men: he knew how to acquire provisions from Geneva or Avignon, bringing
them in by way of Moulins and Roanne, and he could reach the Mediterranean via Nîmes and Montpellier by skirting Burgundian territory. His son
Jacques was the architect of a new power, not only purveyor but banker to the
king, enjoying a monopoly in luxury goods. He equipped the army and provided for the court. Jacques Coeur was the man in charge of the "great ware-

house" that supplied the court's demand for luxuries, the *La Boutique du roi* ("the king's shop"); by calculating his risks he derived enormous profits from it. His rise and power alarmed even the king, who grew jealous and finally overthrew him in order to appropriate his wealth, a tragic story which became very common. It was as if the mechanism whereby the royal finances were privately farmed out necessarily set such events in motion. Louis XII brought down Robertet, who described himself as the only man who did not rob the king, François I overthrew Beaune de Semblançay, and Louis XIV ruined Fouquet. It was the price exacted by absolute monarchy.

Jacques Coeur's *Boutique* followed the court to Touraine, and warehouses were set up in Tours, a prosperous city with healthy finances. On Jacques Coeur's fall, in 1454, his place was taken by an ambitious group of men from that city, his former associates, *notables* (prominent figures in civic government) and merchants who had grown rich.

The businessmen of Tours formed their own association in 1465, and its power continued to expand up to the end of the century. It made fortunes for its members until 1525, a turning point in the reign of François I, marking the end of the Italian campaigns and the court's departure from the banks of the Loire to Paris and Fontainebleau. The heyday of the cities and châteaux of the Loire was over. The end of the Hundred Years War had found Tours particularly well equipped, its well-established civic institutions consolidated by provision for defence. When the city and its wealth had to be protected, walls built and a watch organized, the munificent and public-spirited citizens elected able officials. Tours lived by money changing and the sound currency of the denier tournois. It attracted the merchants and bankers who were gradually replacing the *changeurs*, and were already competing with some of the Lombard financiers. The first Italianate influence to be felt during the Renaissance was undoubtedly financial; politics and architecture followed in its wake.

The *changeur*, the cloth merchant, the financial office-holder and the chief magistrate of the city made up a formidable team, and such men took care to keep their profits in the family. The economy of the most powerful kingdom in Europe became very much a family affair. It was in the hands of the Beaunes, the Briçonnets and the Berthelots, people described by Bernard Chevalier, in his excellent book on the city of Tours at this period,[27] as "the Tours syndicate which exploited the public finances", setting its seal on the collusion between merchants, bankers and office-holders.

When Louis XI made Tours as his favourite city, encouraging its trade and commerce, he depended on these men. They were protected by Jean Bourré, a man in the king's confidence, who helped them to obtain the most lucrative offices, those of the *recette générale de Langue d'Oïl, the chambre aux deniers and the argenterie royale.* The career of Jean Bourré himself, builder of the beautiful château of Le Plessis-Bourré, is typical of the "new lords".[28] Like many of the men with whom the king surrounded himself, he was not of the highest noble birth but came from the *gens de moyen état*, people of middle rank. His father, Guillaume Bourré, was an ordinary bourgeois and a prominent civic figure of Château-Gontier, a man who had made enough money to own a small fief. His mother could claim descent from the minor nobility. Jean Bourré had an uncle who was an abbé and a cousin who was a lieutenant. He studied diligently and learned good Latin, not an unusual accomplishment in a young man whose zeal was stimulated by his modest origins. So he became a secretary: it was from the ranks of such ambitious young men that the king drew his staff, people who would support him against the sons of the great lords. These were the men, citizens and *notables*, notaries, the middle class and merchants, who came to his aid in the struggle against the rebel feudal lords which is known as the *Guerre du Bien Public*, the "War of the Public Good". They struck a tacit bargain with the king: he used their wealth and above all their abilities, in return according them his support, trust and even friendship. Louis XI called his friend Jean Bourré "Maître Jehan of the many skills". Bourré had been secretary to a dauphin in adversity, and rose to prominence when the dauphin became king: he was Secretary to the Great Council, then a Councillor to the king, then *maître des comptes*, then *contrôleur des recettes de Normandie* – this was wealth indeed – and finally *trésorier de France et de l'Ordre de St-Michel*.

Bourré the businessman was also captain of the Château de Langeais, which he rebuilt for the king, besides being governor to the Dauphin Charles and diplomat in extraordinary, frequently dispatched on delicate missions. What qualities, one may ask, brought him all these favours and offices? His competence and his energy, but principally (and the same could be said of the other middle-class men now rising in the world) his total devotion to the service of the king with whom his own fortune was linked. "Sire", Jean Bourré wrote to Louis XI on one occasion, "from the first day I came to you I determined to serve you loyally and to have but one master, and I have always continued in that mind, and now that I am old I would be worse than mad were I to think of doing otherwise".[29]

In a chapter on "The Great Families" in the book cited above, Bernard Chevalier sums up the situation: "This was not a case of an entire class with

Chenonceaux, from the Side of the Château
c. 1513–1522, for Thomas Bohier
Wash drawing, late 16th century

its fortunes on the rise, but of a small group isolating itself in order to succeed in a society where the pre-eminence of the nobility was never questioned".[30] This is the important point about this period of history. Of course, this was the beginning of the bourgeoisie's rise to power. Individual families fell, but the middle class triumphed. It is fair to say that these men sought to rise above the bourgeoisie and never return to it. But perhaps there was, nevertheless, in these remarkable family strategies, some element of "class consciousness"? They certainly dreamed of nothing better than acquiring nobility themselves, and could aspire to no other ideal, but as Chevalier also points out – and it is a striking fact – these rich self-made men did not marry out of their class. None of them "married into" the nobility out of ambition, or acquired nobility by way of a wife's dowry or inheritance. But then again, which party refused such marriages? Certainly, the family policy of the new men was a calculated one, and they adhered to it as rigorously within their own class, one might say their own clan, as the great noble families adhered to it in theirs.

Chevalier emphasizes the fact that "nobility and urban life were radically incompatible". The new men were urban citizens, bourgeois in the etymological sense of the word, and their world was in political and economic contrast to the ethos of the country château that dominated and protected the land around it. We must keep this in mind if we wish to understand the transformation of the fortified castle. The nobility still represented the dominant class, and the assimilation of these newcomers was an experimental and tentative process that came up against barriers social, political, economic and geographical. Apart from marriage, which protected the caste, any means of acquiring noble rank was fair: money, the church, politics and diplomacy, even letters and the arts – even arms. Nobility could be bought, bestowed or conquered: nothing could hold back the new powers determined to infiltrate the aristocracy.

With astonishing, ant-like patience, the rich and powerful Gilles Berthelot acquired tiny parcels of land, adding gradually to the family land at

Azay-le-Rideau that his father Martin had once bought from a certain Bernard. The purchaser of such land bought in debts, exploited the poverty of small landowners, exchanged small properties, and in the end he had his country estate. This was how the Berthelots acquired 387 hectares at Azay and the Bohiers 140 hectares at Chenonceaux. King Louis XII could not refuse such loyal and valued servants the right to make a castellany of their lands – he granted permission for Azay in 1513 and for Chenonceaux in 1514 – and so their fiefdoms were established. Next, as if to confirm his title in everyone's eyes, the new lord immediately built a brand-new château. The haste was significant. The château was the emblem of a very modern kind of success, but the tower at its centre continued to symbolize tradition and privilege.

These new lords sought to emulate the customs of chivalry. Their anxiety to "bear arms" was as significant as the speed with which they built their new châteaux. The chronicler Jean d'Auton describes the scene at the siege of Genoa in April 1507: "In this same hour Messire Charles d'Amboise,

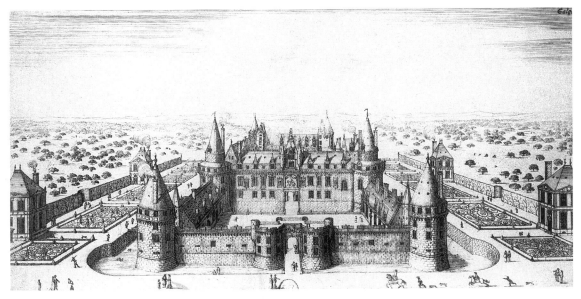

Perspective View of the Château du Verger in Anjou
early 16th century, for the maréchal de Gié
Engraving by Israël Silvestre, mid-17th century

lieutenant-general of the king's army, knighted one Maistre Thomas Bouyer, *général* of Normandy, who was there in the camp fully armed, clad in a fine tunic of cloth of gold, and mounted on his courser".[31] Another writer tells us how, at Marignano in 1515, Thomas Bohier, Antoine Duprat and Guillaume de Beaune "were on the field that evening when the alarm was given, and were in arms near the rearguard, being good men of means and good servants of the king".[32]

Such men were not generals but controllers general. They were nonetheless happy to mix with the real soldiers and emulate them. If you had money, a military career offered considerable opportunities for rising in the social scale, ever if it was a career best suited to men of noble birth. In fact the other important builders of the time were the great military leaders, not all of them nobly born, but chosen by the king for their courage and zeal in his Italian campaigns. The Château d'Argy still contains a fine pillared gallery which is a reasonably faithful replica of the gallery in the Louis XII wing at Blois: it was commissioned by one of the king's lieutenants, Charles de Brillac, killed at Milan in 1509 during the Italian campaign.

The maréchal de Gié, Cardinal d'Amboise and Admiral de Bonnivet were the other great builders of this period. The first distinguished himself fighting beside Charles VIII in the Neapolitan campaign, became governor of the Château d'Amboise, and built the Château du Verger and the Château de Mortier-Crolles. The second, who was first minister to Louis XII and in 1507 accompanied the king to Genoa, where he was victorious, was appointed viceroy of the duchy of Milan and nearly became pope, and built the Château de Gaillon. The third, commander-in-chief of François I's armies, conducted the king's negotiations for election as Holy Roman Emperor at the Diet of Frankfurt in 1519, and the negotiations at the Field of the Cloth of Gold for the Dauphin's marriage to Mary Tudor. He built the Château de Bonnivet in Poitou, now destroyed.

These newly enriched financiers, soldiers and ecclesiastics were great builders. The financiers among them were townsmen, prominent figures in civic life and urban builders before they began building in the country. Consequently the cities of the Loire – Saumur, Tours, Amboise, Blois, Beaugency, Orléans – acquired renovated *hôtels de ville* (town halls) and magnificent town houses, many of them still standing today. In 1451 François Doulcet, who had become *Maître de la Chambre aux deniers* to Louis XII, began work on the Château de Beauregard in the forest of Blois. The Morvilliers, who built their town house in the rue Pierre de Blois, were cloth merchants; one of them was municipal magistrate in 1455. A century later a member of the same family was bishop of Orléans and keeper of the seals of Henri II. Another house in the same street belonged to Villebrême, secretary to Marie de Clèves and founder of yet another dynasty, like the Phelippeaux family of Blois, which continued to provide secretaries of state as late as the eighteenth century. The Phelippeaux had a mansion in town and a château at Herbault, not far from Chambord. Pierre de Refuge, owner of the Château de Fougères-sur-Bièvre, was a country squire who rose to become Charles VII's *général des finances* of Outre-Seine-et-Yonne in 1457, and was then *général des finances* of Languedoc and Langue d'Oïl from 1469 to 1473 under Louis XI, and *gouverneur des finances* to the duc d'Orléans. Cottereau, who held the post of *maître des eaux et forêts*, built the Hôtel de Jassaud, which still stands in the rue Fontaine-des-Elus.

The most extraordinary of these success stories is the career of Florimond Robertet, Louis XII's great financier. He built a magnificent mansion in the city, rivalling the king's new buildings themselves – a visit to the rue St-Honoré enables one to compare them – and two leagues away he also built the vast Château de Bury, the most modern château in the kingdom in 1515, with Michelangelo's famous statue of David in its central courtyard.

The city of Tours was also adorned with new mansions built by the new lords. The largest of them was the house of Jacques de Beaune de Semblançay. Nothing of it now remains except part of the wall at the corner of the rue Colbert and the rue Nationale, but it is sufficient evidence of the building's extraordinary quality and modernity: the wall, now isolated, remains a lesson in architecture. Great casements determine the clarity and lightness of the general effect, which is rigorously and harmoniously conceived, with fine Italianate ornamentation. The "de Beaune Fountain" in front of the house, with its airy arabesques, was directly inspired by Italy. Although the *hôtel de ville* of Tours, like its counterpart in Blois, has completely disappeared, other buildings which have survived destruction and restoration, chiefly those standing near the cathedral of St Martin, still suggest, as Paul Vitry puts it, "that in the past, from the fifteenth to the eighteenth century, this was an almost aristocratic quarter, or at least a quarter where the *grande bourgeoisie* lived."[3] Doors with ogee arches, little courtyards surrounded by galleries of pointed segmental arcades, staircase turrets outside the main part of the building all follow one another in close succession, signs of wealth if not nobility. It was here that the Briçonnet, Berthelot and Bohier families had their private houses. Their own mansions have gone, but the magnificent Hôtel Gouïn still stands at the corner of the rue du Commerce and the rue Bouchereau. We do not know who built it; its name is that of a later owner. Its north façade is that of a plain, even austere late fifteenth-century manor house, while the south side, looking out on the courtyard, is profusely adorned with early Renaissance ornamentation. From the breast-walls to the high pediments of the gable windows, bas-relief decoration entirely covers the narrow façade in ostentatious display. The owners of these proudly ornamented houses – wealthy craftsmen, goldsmiths or bankers – have fallen into oblivion, but the names of the streets where the buildings stand retain their significance. One of the finest of these mansions displays its wooden sculptures like figureheads on the corner of the rue du Change and rue de la Monnaie.

Bourges (Cher)
Hôtel Jacques Coeur, 1443–1453

ABOVE LEFT:
Tympanum of door on the north staircase,
overlooking the courtyard
ABOVE RIGHT, RIGHT,
AND FACING PAGE ABOVE:
Decorated window bases, main staircase
overlooking the courtyard
FACING PAGE BELOW:
Interior courtyard and open gallery

The town mansion

… The Hôtel Jacques Coeur, built at a time when the King of France was known as "the King of Bourges"; architecture in the grand style in the home of a rich bourgeois…

LEFT:
Château de Fougères-sur-Bièvre
Begun 1475–1520, originally built
for Pierre de Refuge
Gallery of the interior courtyard,
1510–1520

BELOW:
Château de Talcy
Begun 1520 for Bernard Salviati
Interior courtyard

Built on the royal model

… The architecture of the royal palace was imitated by its satellite châteaux, prefiguring the "court" that formed around the absolute monarch …

Château d'Argy
mid-14th century, rebuilt for the de
Brillac family
Residence of Charles de Brillac, pre-1509
Galleries, north and west wings

RIGHT:
Jacques Androuet du Cerceau
Les plus Excellents Bastiments de France,
1576–1579
Château de Bury
1511–1515, for Florimond Robertet
Elevation of the entrance side

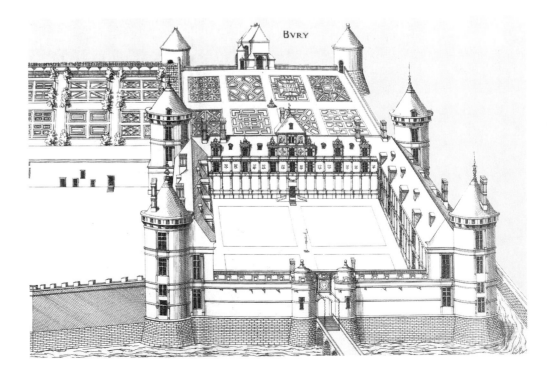

Country houses and town houses

… The *nouveaux riches* were not landed gentry; they built châteaux in order to appear noble, but their main residences were in the heart of the commercial city …

Blois (Loir-et-Cher)
Hôtel d'Alluye
1508, for Florimond Robertet, baron d'Alluye

<small>RIGHT AND
FACING PAGE ABOVE:</small>
Interior courtyard and galleries
<small>ABOVE:</small>
Bay window in the east wing

A new style of ornamentation in prosperous cities

… It was in the cities that real architectural innovations were made, rather than in the châteaux, which were still restricted to the mediaeval model. In Tours the new architecture is seen at its best in the cloisters of the collegiate church of St Martin, or on the façade of the Hôtel de Beaune, shown opposite…

Blois (Loir-et-Cher)
Hôtel Salviati, late 15th century

ABOVE:
Loggia overlooking the courtyard
FACING PAGE ABOVE LEFT:
Elevation of the façade, wash drawing,
late 19th century

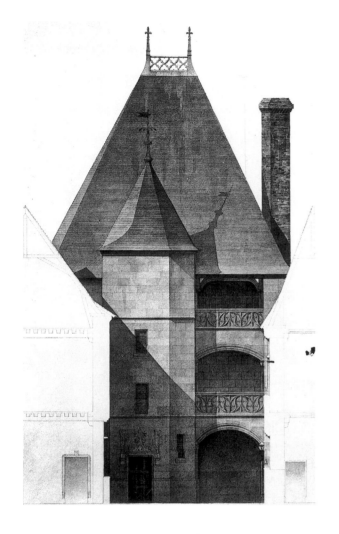

ABOVE RIGHT AND RIGHT:
Tours (Indre-et-Loire)
Hôtel de Beaune-Semblançay
1510–1518, for Jacques de
Beaune
Details of the façade of the
main building

Tours (Indre-et-Loire)
Hôtel Gouïn, late 15th to early 16th century

ABOVE:
Entrance porch
RIGHT, BELOW AND
FACING PAGE ABOVE:
Details, decorated window bases
FACING PAGE BELOW:
South façade, c. 1510

Refinement:
The private town house

… Besides châteaux and churches, formerly the only kind of architecture built in stone and for display, fine civic buildings and bourgeois houses were now erected in the reconstructed streets of the cities of the Loire valley …

Beaugency (Loiret)
Hôtel de Ville, built from 1525
Street façade

ABOVE:
First-floor windows
FACING PAGE:
Entrance porch

ABOVE:
Saumur (Maine-et-Loire)
Hôtel de Ville, early 16th century
Façade seen from the banks of the Loire

LEFT:
Loches (Indre-et-Loire)
Hôtel de Ville, 1535–1543
Façade in the place of the Hôtel de Ville,
and the 15th-century Picois gate

The Hôtel de Ville: An expression of power

… Characteristic of municipal organization, which had been consolidated by the war, was the emergence of an urban style of architecture squares, streets and fountains – and above all the building of those fine hôtels de ville erected by all the cities of the Loire in the second half of the fifteenth century …

5

Azay-le-Rideau, a Model

The finances of the state had become the province of a select group of families. Gilles Berthelot was born into one of them. The history of the Berthelot fortune went back to his grandfather, Jean, one of the bourgeois of Tours who were summoned by Charles VII to sit in the Parlement of Paris when in 1436, after winning back his capital, he had to rebuild a loyal administration there, one in line with the new shape of society.

Jean Berthelot was one of Charles VII's councillors, and became treasurer to Louis XI and *maître de la chambre aux deniers*: that is to say, he was in charge of the king's privy purse. His son Martin held the same appointments under Louis XII. It is interesting to note, in passing, the remarkably consistent royal policy; quarrels and radical differences of temperament there might be, but inherited competence often guaranteed the perennity of an alliance.

Gilles Berthelot, son of Martin and grandson of Jean, amassed many offices and honours under Louis XII and François I, and it was with this money and the fortune of his wife, Philippe Lesbahy, that the Château d'Azay-le-Rideau was built.[34]

Gilles had three aunts, Jeanne, Marie and Gilenne. Jeanne was the mother of Guillaume Briçonnet, a great builder; he became s*urintendant des finances* (chief minister of finance) and a cardinal, organized Charles VIII's Italian campaigns, and crowned Louis XII. Marie married into the Fumée family: her son Adam was keeper of the seals. Gilenne married into the Ruzé family, and her daughter Jeanne was the wife of the famous Jacques de Beaune de Semblançay, one of the richest men in France and the king's banker. As a result, a considerable part of the kingdom's wealth was concentrated in the five families of Berthelot, Fumée, Ruzé, Briçonnet and de Beaune. Before Guillaume Briçonnet took orders and became a cardinal he was married to the sister of Jacques de Beaune de Semblançay. The cardinal had a daughter from this marriage, Catherine Briçonnet, who married Thomas Bohier, another prominent figure in Tours and the builder of Chenonceaux. Chenonceaux and Azay-le-Rideau were thus closely linked, and the two châteaux, like the men who ordered their construction, may be described as first cousins.

At the beginning of his reign François I consolidated and even increased the power of the men of Tours: in 1517 Jacques de Beaune de Semblançay was appointed to the post of *surintendant et gouverneur général des finances* left vacant by Briçonnet on his death in 1514. Gilles Berthelot became third president of the Parlement and one of the four *trésoriers de France*. When Thomas Bohier left for Milan, Berthelot filled his post as *général des finances* for Normandy. The lands of Azay-le-Rideau had become the property of two families: the family of Martin Berthelot, father of Gilles, and the family of Antoine Lesbahy, another rich bourgeois, who had an only daughter named Philippe, a cultivated and strong-minded woman. A man called Janet du Bois-Jourdain, lord of Azay, still owed the Lesbahys three hundred livres. Gilles Berthelot tried to purchase this debt. The accounts for the business procedures involved, conducted in Chinon, Loudun and Tours, have been preserved, so that we know everything about them down to the eight sols eight deniers spent by a messenger at an inn.[35] This inheritance was Philippe's dowry. The marriage was celebrated in 1518, and work began the same year on the new château of Azay-le-Rideau. It was to be built over the remains of an old manor on an island in the Indre.

What kind of château did the Berthelots set out to build? It was to be a perfect quadrilateral with four turrets, no longer massive watch-towers but smaller, decorative turrets of the *échauguette* type built at the angles of the building, as at Chenonceaux, with tall roofs in the French style correctly set above a parapet walk with machicolations.

The great tower of the old manor of Azay was preserved, and the château was still to be surrounded by water like a fortified castle. Indeed, it was built on the bed of the Indre itself. These traditional features, however, were softened by a great deal of fine, elegant ornamentation, by the symmetry and regularity of the outline, and finally by a straight staircase, its wide landings opening on a series of bays.

The château owed much to tradition, to the current idea of the Italian style, and finally to Chenonceaux, where building had begun between 1514 and 1515. No expense was spared at Azay-le-Rideau. Gilles Berthelot was at the zenith of his career. Work went ahead very quickly, and the harmony which still delights visitors today was the product of that rapidity, for Azay has the advantage of being a homogeneous building, unusual when châteaux were often rebuilt ten times over. The staircase was already being built in 1524, and we know how quickly it was constructed from two account books which have fortunately been preserved in the archives of Indre-et-Loire. They show what large sums were laid out in the interests of speed.[36]

Philippe Lesbahy supervised the building herself; she seems to have been the person who commissioned work in her husband's absence, and he is not mentioned in the accounts. On 12 June 1518, however, she had to go to Angers, and she left the task of "supervising the accounts for the building of the château of Azay" to a man she trusted: Guillaume Artault, Abbé de St-Cyr. It was no light responsibility. As many as 131 labourers were employed, along with 13 masons and 7 carpenters, working day and night on the foundations. They were paid fifteen deniers for day shifts and twenty for night shifts; obviously the Berthelots were not going to stint on the forces they employed. The first problem to be solved was draining the river Indre on the site of the château so that the foundations could be laid, and the first sums expended were for "removing the waters and soil for the foundations". The following year, on 10 July 1519, a further sum was entered for "removing the waters and soil to make certain foundations", and a contract with a drainage expert from Tours, Etienne Turmeau, was signed before a notary; he was to undertake drainage work before the walls of "the red chamber" were underpinned. Pumps were installed the length of the building site for the purpose. The accounts record: "To Jean de la Croix, for two days spent with Thoreau le Maroy setting up the pumps … paid to the pumpman to make ready the pumps …". Work did not stop in winter, and there were payments for "sixteen pairs of gloves for the masons", and to "the shoemaker for repairing the boots of the said masons". Makers of buckets and wheelbarrows, men who dressed skins and men who repaved pickaxes were all employed. The bulk of the expenditure, however, was on building materials and the cost of transporting them along the river to the site.

The site foreman in charge of the works seems to have been the master mason Denis Gillonet. He had been brought from Paris and was paid large sums of money, out of which he may have paid his own assistants: Pierre Rousseau, described as a "master mason", although he received a hundred livres directly from Philippe Lesbahy, Etienne Rousseau, Pierre Maupoint, and others. Philippe Lesbahy also brought a carpenter called Thierry from Paris. Another carpenter, Jacques Thoreau, cut and squared timber "to make props to shore up the walls". This wood was not for the timbers of the building itself but for use as scaffolding, and in particular for the piles and casings essential in work on such marshy ground. Jean Marcasseau was paid for

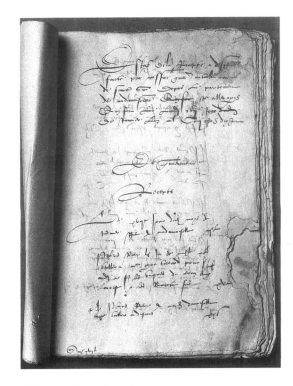

Château d'Azay-le-Rideau
Account book for the building of the château, 1518–1519

working "in his capacity as joiner on items for the said master mason, in making him several casings".

A second book, also kept by Guillaume Artault from January to August 1519, when Philippe Lesbahy was away again, in Paris, shows how fast the work was progressing: it mentions Pierre Maupoint as a "sculptor" as well as a mason, and many deliveries of stone were being made.

During the 1520s, the kingdom's financial difficulties worsened, particularly at the court of François I. His treasury was bled dry by his opulent retinue and building projects at Blois and Chambord, but most of all by his Italian campaigns, diplomatic activities in Europe and ambition to be Emperor. The more exorbitant the requirements of this dispendious king, the greater the power of the financiers became. Gilles Berthelot was given the job of levying a new tax devised by himself: *amortissement*, "amortization", to be charged on all Church property. This tax involved a huge risk for an equally huge gain. In fact, not only did the Church represent an almost unlimited reservoir of funds, but the rate of the new tax was never fixed, so the *trésorier* could fix his own terms with his rich ecclesiastical taxpayers.

It is easy to see the margin of personal profit this latitude allowed him.

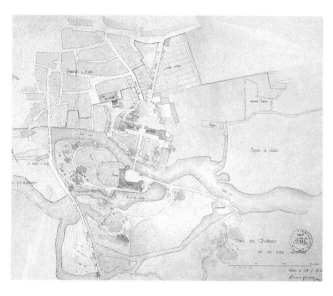

Azay-le-Rideau (Indre-et-Loire)
Drawn by J. Hardion
Plan showing situation of the town and the château, 1904–1906

However, it laid the man holding the post open to the hostility of all the great Church proprietors, and they were powerful people. Consequently, the financiers played on both popular hatred for the churchmen and the envy of them felt by the kings whose destiny they controlled. The ecclesiastics resisted the first but bowed to the second, since they could do nothing about it. Repeated setbacks in the war made matters difficult: in mid-campaign, the army commanders complained of lack of money, ascribing their defeats to the diversion of funds, for which they held the financiers to blame. The financiers were ostentatiously building châteaux, while mercenary soldiers disbanded for lack of pay. The great military commanders Lautrec, Bayard and Bonnivet laid complaints against Semblançay, the most powerful of those financiers. On 11 March 1524 an examination of his accounts was ordered. Semblançay sensed danger in the air; so did his family, and so did Gilles Berthelot, who was encountering resistance in his attempts to levy the amortization tax at a time when the staircase and upper parts of his château of Azay were being built. In spite of these difficulties François I set off campaigning in Italy again, but for the last time: he was defeated and taken prisoner at Pavia in 1525.

Pavia is a major landmark in the long reign of François I. At this point the building sites on the Loire were abandoned: first of all the royal buildings, for after his return from captivity the king did not stay there for such long periods as before, then the buildings of the Tours financiers, since the military defeat at Pavia was the signal for their own downfall. On 3 January 1527, as soon as François I was back from captivity, Semblançay was thrown into the Bastille and condemned to death. Whether or not he was genuinely guilty hardly matters, although the king's mother, Louise de Savoie, blamed him for all her son's misfortunes. As we have seen, the organization of the royal finances could hardly have been operated by innocents, but in this case Semblançay was made a scapegoat, and the people knew it. A pardon was expected to arrive, even at the foot of the scaffold, where he awaited execution for six hours. The pardon never came. Semblançay's son immediately fled to Cologne, and his wife was imprisoned. Gilles Berthelot, who had no doubt tried to defend him, swiftly took refuge in Metz, and he died at Cambrai, still in exile, two years later. Azay-le-Rideau was unfinished, and unfinished it remained: it was half of a château with two wings at right angles, never to be joined. The façade still shows the scar left when building work stopped. On either side of the scar, the similarity between the stonework and the ornamentation suggests that work on the unfinished château must have quickly resumed, at least in order to complete it provisionally. François I confiscated it for the benefit of one of his captains, Antoine Raffin, who did not continue the work. The king was still claiming the sum of 49,399 livres from Gilles Berthelot for maladministration. Philippe Lesbahy fought doughtily, bringing legal proceedings herself until 1532, and she did not make terms until 1563, when she was an old woman. Work on the financier's château came to as sudden an end as its owner's dazzling career.

Thus preserved in its wounded state, with the evidence of its rapid construction almost intact, the château has a slightly ingenuous freshness, undisturbed by the alterations wrought by restorers and the passage of time. Even today, it offers the image of a model château, the archetypal château of the Loire. Azay-le-Rideau is one of the first buildings where the desire for symmetry in the façades was the overriding principle of design. If it had been finished its symmetrical regularity would have enhanced the impression of balance and calm, and perhaps dispelled some of the picturesque charm generated by the imbalance in the two wings. The great staircase would have been situated in the middle of the north façade (since the last tier of windows

Château d'Azay-le-Rideau
1518–1527
Capital of a pilaster, north façade

on the left as you face the building from the court would have been occupied by the adjoining wing), precisely on the axis of the entrance.

As for the entrance wing itself, we do not know how it would have looked; perhaps a plain gallery, as Jean Guillaume suggests,[37] imitating the most modern designs of the time at Blois and Bury, or perhaps a more military type of postern in keeping with the great tower. Since that tower was preserved at the price of an oblique adjustment to the line of the north wall, showing what importance was attached to its conservation, and since the builders took such care over equilibrium that they could hardly have left that portion of the north wing without something to match it on the other side, the second hypothesis seems most likely. This suggests that the mere presence of the great tower determined the design of this hypothetical wing, and that just enough space was left for an exact replica to be built to the east.

If the master of works on the site was to retain the mathematical regularity of the façades, he had to cheat with the windows, something often done in later classical architecture. On the west façade, the penultimate of the five tiers of windows was situated precisely on the axis of the main wall of the north façade, so that they open not into a room but on to a wall. This absurdity was preferred to a jarring irregularity in the west façade, where the three casements of each of the five tiers of windows are reflected in the moat, impeccably aligned one above another. In the same façade, the gateway looking out on the water – suggesting that a bridge might have been added – is not centrally placed on this façade but corresponds to the ornamented gateway leading to the courtyard on the other side of the building, which is situated in the very centre of the wing as it appears from the courtyard. The master of works was obviously striving for consistent visual regularity as the symbol of a world of order and equilibrium.

A satisfying equilibrium was certainly achieved at Azay-le-Rideau in one respect. The dormer windows rise straight from the façade, neither set back from the parapet walk, which would have meant an awkward break in the crown it forms (as at Le Lude), nor emerging from the roof after an interruption to the vertical line (as at Valençay). The machicolations consequently run uninterrupted all around the outside of the façades without affecting the verticals, following the model of the Château de Gaillon where superimposed pilasters were used for the first time – a felicitous Italianate variation on the many little columns along Gothic walls – and rejecting the example set by the François I façade at Blois, where the heavily ornamented cornice masks the lower parts of the dormers.

The unity, simplicity and clarity of the design resolved the difficult problem always associated with the upper parts of such buildings, since the horizontal bands emphasizing each level run unbroken all around the château, and similarly the vertical tiers seem to spring in a single movement from the ground floor to the pediments of the dormers. These vertical lines are accented at close quarters by discreet pilasters, and from a distance by the tall roofs of the turrets, each of which has a tall window and is capped by a slender metal finial. The château, like a work of sculpture, gives an impression of airy, calculated and controlled equilibrium, and this impression is reinforced by one final detail: the relatively moderate use of the Italian ornamentation so fashionable at the time, both in the Loire region and further afield. Flamboyant art with its wealth of decoration, a style reinforced by the equally heavily ornamented Italian bas-reliefs of the period after 1500, was in evidence at Gaillon and Meillant, even at Tours in the excessive foliated decoration on the façades of the Hôtel Gouïn. At Azay, ornamentation is kept for the crucial points – the monumental staircase which is the pivot of the whole work, the doors, and to some extent the pilasters of the windows – and then emerges joyously, so to speak, in the highest parts of the building, those furthest removed from the eye, the pediments of the dormers. The balance between the plain and ornamented areas is as effective as the balance between the tiers of windows and the vertical spaces between them: neither dominates the other, and the eye is led alternately to each.

Azay-le-Rideau is famous for its elegance today: we may seek the explanation not only in the clarity of its design, with its perfect adjustment of empty and occupied spaces, of horizontals and verticals, but in the circumstances of its construction. The work was done fast and all of a piece, so that the whole building conveys a sense of unity un-impaired by its nineteenth-century restoration. Unlike Chenonceaux, which has a bridge entirely out of keeping with the rest of it, and unlike almost all the other châteaux with their disparate wings, reconstructed over the centuries and often producing a bizarre or fantastic appearance, Azay is a rare example of a homogeneous building, and the idea behind it has remained intact, even if the stones themselves have not.

The approach to Azay-le-Rideau

… Nestling in a valley, the château owes nothing to its mediaeval
site but a pleasant setting. There is no defensive element in its present
surroundings: instead of the stagnant waters of a moat with a glacis,
the river laps around it, a peaceful waterway that once conveyed great
wealth …

Château d'Azay-le-Rideau
1518–1527, built for Gilles Berthelot

FACING PAGE:
Banks of the river Indre
ABOVE:
Approach to the château, looking towards
the axis of the great staircase

Château d'Azay-le-Rideau, 1518–1527

LEFT:
Turret at the south-west corner
FACING PAGE:
View of the east façade

RIGHT:
Château d'Azay-le-Rideau, 1518–1527
Ground-floor plan
Wash drawing by J. Hardion, 1904–1906

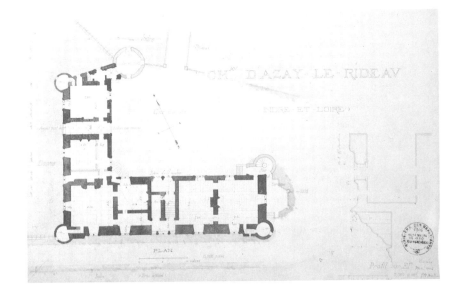

The plan of the château with its angle towers

… Closed in on itself, graciously unfolding only within its shell, the plan is still a military one, but the military element is symbolic: the main building is more important than the towers, which embellish rather than flank the angles, with the exception of the keep, which was associated with the privileges of nobility …

The organization of the façade

… The strongly emphasized verticals of the religious and military tradition are now counter-balanced by horizontal lines which seem to be trying to hold the château down to earth, evoking its owner's prosperity as much as any flights of spirituality …

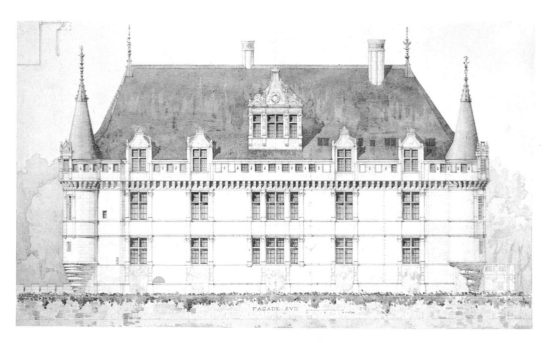

Château d'Azay-le-Rideau, 1518–1527

Facing Page:
West façade
Above:
South façade
Left:
South façade
Wash drawing by J. Hardion, 1904–1906

The design

… The key points: Graphic care is taken to rationalize the ornamentation, which is lavished solely on the door and window frames and roof level. The façade can be read like a book, with its frontispiece, ornamental bands, capital letters and margins, anticipating later classical theories …

Château d'Azay-le-Rideau, 1518–1527

FACING PAGE ABOVE:
South-east angle turret, detail
ABOVE AND FACING PAGE BELOW:
South façade, details
LEFT:
South-west angle turret, cul-de-lampe

Château d'Azay-le-Rideau, 1518–1527
North façade, the great staircase overlooking the courtyard

<small>LEFT AND FACING PAGE BELOW:</small>
Canopied niches, details of ornamentation
<small>BELOW:</small>
Double windows on the first floor
<small>FACING PAGE ABOVE:</small>
View looking up at the staircase façade

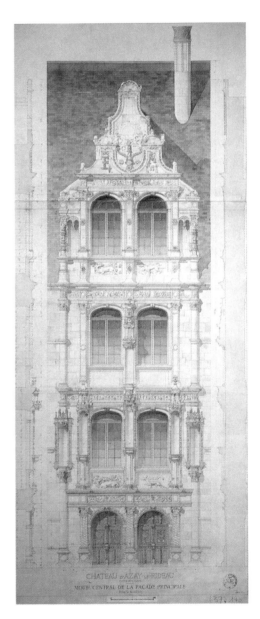

<small>ABOVE:</small>
Château d'Azay-le-Rideau
Elevation of staircase
Wash drawing by J. Hardion

The staircase

… The stairway is a bravura flourish in the architecture of the châteaux of the Loire. It is rich in symbolism rather than functional, the dramatic illustration of a calculated ascent, it is the axis around which the whole building is organized …

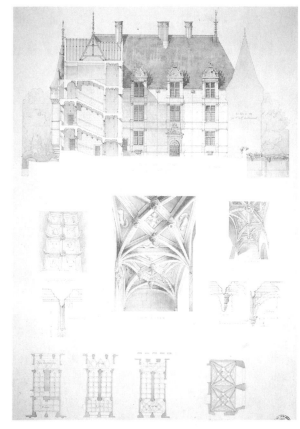

Château d'Azay-le-Rideau, 1518–1527
Interior of the great staircase

ABOVE LEFT:
Detail of handrail
ABOVE RIGHT:
Section of the staircase, with plans and details
Wash drawing by J. Hardion
RIGHT:
Vaulted ceiling on the fourth landing of the
staircase
FACING PAGE:
First flight of the staircase

… The staircase provides access to the interior of the building through
what seems a triumphal arch. The stairwell, the building's main vertical
axis of movement, has wide bays opening to the exterior, and its
ornamentation is particularly rich and elegant …

Ornamentation of the doors and window frames

… On the façade, ornamentation is confined to the openings –
the door and window frames – and the cornices; here, the decorative
extravagance of Flamboyant architecture is kept within bounds.
Though restrained, the motifs are those of a chivalric, warrior society …

Château d'Azay-le-Rideau, 1518–1527
Doors

FACING PAGE ABOVE:
Doorway to stair of the keep
FACING PAGE BELOW:
Doors leading to the great staircase
ABOVE:
Door in the west façade, overlooking
the moat
RIGHT:
Door in the east façade, opening onto
the courtyard

The dormers

… While Flamboyant ornamentation showing some Italian influence is used in moderation on the façades, it is lavished on the dormers. Of exaggerated size, they extend the vertical dimension of the building as if to crown it …

The roofs

…The roofs finials pointing upward to the sky confer on the private château a distinction till then confined to churches. The French tradition of "elevation" is maintained, but power has changed hands, and the finials symbolise not spiritual aspiration but upward mobility…

Château d'Azay-le-Rideau, 1518–1527

<small>ABOVE AND RIGHT:</small>
Finials of the roof
<small>FACING PAGE:</small>
South-east angle turret; details of the roof

6

VARIATIONS

Azay-le-Rideau is not the first, the most modern or the largest among all the new and rival buildings of the time, but it provides the best illustration of the main characteristics of this type of architecture in its heyday. It presents itself to us, in the words of Jean Guillaume, as an "ideal building, a perfect summary of the new concept of French architecture as it existed in the king's entourage in Touraine around 1520".[38]

First, the date of its construction sets it at the heart of the great architectural period of the early Renaissance: after the first major experiments in the modernization of the château, at Gaillon, which was completed in 1510, and at Le Verger and Bury, built between 1511 and 1515, the masons of the Loire were ready to put into practice the ideas brought back to them by travellers who had visited Italy. Those travellers, including the king himself, had been to Naples, Milan and Pavia. The Loire valley masons knew about these places, but only from hearsay – almost no architectural treatises had yet been translated into French, and no doubt a number of the masons could not have read them anyway, or at least were not theoreticians.

The years between 1515 and 1519 were the most favourable for architecture. François I was a young, rich and enterprising king, and aspired to be Holy Roman Emperor until the failure of his election campaign in 1519 (a failure which began the decline of his fortune and his reputation). Building on Chenonceaux, to a determinedly original plan, began about 1513. At Bonnivet, where work began in 1516, the arrangement of the tiers and the placing of a staircase with double bays in the middle of the façade were part of a design which was the direct predecessor of Azay-le-Rideau. At the same time the king was adorning the last wing to be rebuilt in his château of Blois with loggias and a dramatic staircase. In 1519, after abandoning the grandiose projects devised for his château of Romorantin by Leonardo da Vinci, who died at Amboise that year (in the king's arms, according to legend), he began to build Chambord, although he was never to finish it.

A feature in common to these and many other châteaux was the advantage they derived both from the technical expertise of the craftsmen who built them, an expertise encouraged and cultivated by the prosperity of France over the previous fifty years, and from the new ideas adopted by a spirit of enterprise that was military and political in the case of the kings, and commercial and financial in the case of the bankers.

It is quite likely that the palaces of Venice, surrounded by canals, with galleries opening out on the water, were the model for Chenonceaux, as Jean Guillaume has ingeniously argued.[39] However, the bold plan of building a château on the piers of a mill, so that it was actually situated over the riverbed, also coincided with the old custom of surrounding fortified castles with moats or building them on easily defensible peninsulas. Azay-le-Rideau on its island thus combined beauty with tradition and utility – for the river provided access. Although the basic idea is not the same, there is a considerable resemblance between the deep moat still to be seen today at the Château du Moulin near Romorantin, and the artificial canals with which Leonardo da Vinci proposed to surround the king's châteaux at Romorantin itself. Today we admire the quiet waters of the wide moat reflecting the château of Le Plessis-Bourré, although it originally must have been intended as a fortification. Such ambiguities are very much in the spirit of this period of the Renaissance, when the upper classes were conspicuous consumers of the wealth obtained from a modern economy. It is interesting that the financiers who built Chenonceaux and d'Azay preferred running water to the stagnant moat which had formerly surrounded fortified castles: the river was a better symbol of their taste for the free circulation of goods.

The ambiguity of its functions was displayed no less in the plan of châteaux than in their siting. Traditionally, châteaux were polygons flanked by towers. The single massive building of Chenonceaux, built without wings, and with towers shrunk to the size of turrets at its corners, was certainly an innovation, but the usual fortified-castle pattern found at Chaumont, Ussé, Le Verger and Bury was still followed at Azay. Leonardo da Vinci, working for Charles d'Amboise in Milan, knew no other pattern, and Chambord was eventually built in accordance with the old tradition, although a wooden model, known to us only from hearsay and a drawing, did represent a single massive building with internal divisions, like Chenonceaux and the châteaux soon to be built in the classical style.[40]

Towers were built lower now, but the smaller and more elegant pepper-pot turrets that took their place were still part of the mediaeval repertory. On the other hand the square pavilion was a genuine architectural mutation, a military tower that had become a pleasure-pavilion; it could be seen in the middle of the central wing at Bury and at the corners of the building at Villesavin, a small château in the modern style built by the superintendent of building works at Chambord on the edge of the park in 1537. Where fortified wings still existed, their effect was almost always lighter than before. They became galleries, prudently open only on the courtyard side at first, at Bury and in the Louis XII wing at Blois, or perched on the terrace at Gaillon, but soon they opened out still further until, at Villesavin again and at Gué-Péan,[41] they all but ceased to exist. This development anticipated the château without either courtyard or tower, a simple right-angled pavilion like the hunting lodge Du Thier began rebuilding as a château at Beauregard, near Blois, in 1545. In view of all the possibilities these new ideas offered to architects, it is difficult to construct any theory of what Azay would have looked like if it had been completed. In principle, the strong vertical emphasis in the elevations is a feature of traditional French architecture, both military and religious. However, the care taken to impose regularity (with partial success at Bonnivet and almost perfect success at Azay-le-Rideau) is part of a new movement. The dramatic unity of the façades depends on tiers, vertical sections emphasized by conspicuous structures and is further enhanced by pointed dormer windows with pinnacles or lanterns beside them.

The space allotted to the dormers, which are so characteristic of fifteenth-century French châteaux and correspond to the extravagant gables over the portals of Flamboyant churches, serves no purpose: it was the result of a drive towards elevation, an aesthetic deriving from ecclesiastical architecture as much as from the defensive requirements which had concentrated the more spectacular parts of the château at the top of its towers. The result was fortifications adorned with airy superstructures full of windows and lacy ornamentation. A glance at the Château de l'Islette, near Azay-le-Rideau, where the dormers have been removed and the roof-line brought down level with the top of the façade wall, shows the disastrous effect of such amputation.

The châteaux of this period, up to an including Chambord, still display strong vertical movement. The effect is produced by tiers of windows rising from the ground floor up, with fillets between the floors, leading the eye up to the roof and the top of the dormer. The dormers at Azay-le-Rideau are extremely enlarged; this role is played at Chambord and – in almost exaggerated fashion – at Villegongis by the chimneys ranged along the very steep roofs, which are described as *à la française* because they are so very much a part of this particular tradition.

The innovative feature of the châteaux of the Loire, anticipating future architectural styles, was the way in which this quasi-sublimated vertical effect, characteristic of Flamboyant art, found its counterpoint in the systematic imposition of horizontals. These horizontals seem to be trying to keep the château earthbound, establishing lines which would gradually become dominant in civil architecture, and which reflect the prosperous and comfortable life of the building's proprietor rather than any ascendant movement of spirituality or absolutism. The underlying pattern of the new aesthetic coincided with the rising power of the French financiers: it can be seen in the mansion – indeed almost an urban château – that Jacques Coeur built himself in Bourges in the mid-fifteenth century, where the floor levels are horizontally marked by fillets of decoration in relief. The need to balance the vertical and the horizontal, instructive in financiers, came to be seen as a virtue by politicians too. François Gebelin correctly ascribes major significance to the horizontal banding typical of the façades of the châteaux of the Loire. Symptomatic as it was, however, it caused no revolution in architecture and remained very much a surface matter – proof, if any is needed, of its essentially symbolic character.

Most of the Loire châteaux illustrate this tendency to give symbolic prominence to features that might otherwise have passed unnoticed; the appearance of rationality that results is purely aesthetic. This emphasis on ideal and systematic reason in architecture was very new, and anticipated classical ideas. Previously, the internal arrangements had determined those

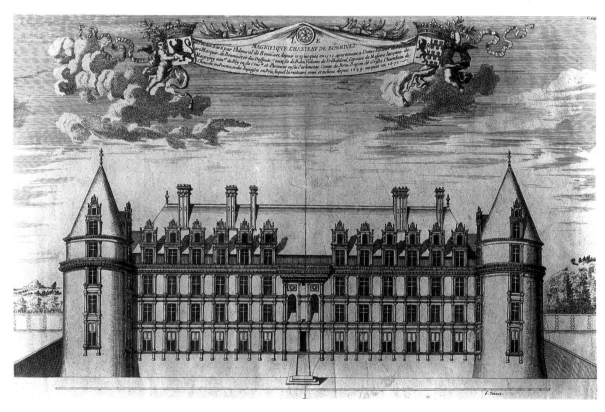

F. de la Pointe, after François de la Guertière
Château de Bonnivet
Begun 1516, for Admiral de Bonnivet
Engraving, late 17th century

of the façade; now the façade took priority, imposing a linear arrangement of rooms on the interior, and if necessary employing a *trompe l'œil* effect to complete a symmetrical set of tiers. The château was literally "squared up". As a result, possibilities inside were limited and the plan was reduced to a simple succession of large rooms, often quite undifferentiated. The kitchen, the salon, the chamber and the antechamber followed one another on the same level, so that the château as a whole was reduced, in turn, to a mere instrument of display, unsuitable for any specific function and, in particular, for use as a dwelling. Its idealized structure was chiefly a setting for parades, hunting, festivities and the reception of guests; it was not a place to live in. Indeed the requirements of ordinary life would not have fitted into the rigorous, elementary lines of the design. Sometimes the masons of the Loire had difficulty in mastering this rigorous style – it is merely suggested at Blois, and at Bonnivet, according to Jean Guillaume, the façade was regular only in the drawing which is all that remains of it[42], while we have already seen that at Azay-le-Rideau a tier of windows opens on to a wall. However, the mason's clumsiness in the planning department was more likely to produce innovation than their impeccable mastery of stonework, in which generations of practice had made them virtuoso. This also transpires in their courageous efforts to change the design of staircases, and the errors which resulted in the occasional non-coincidence of landings and floors (as in the admittedly unassuming private house built in Blois, No. 7 rue Porte Chartraine) were a better indication of future trends than the perfect spirals climbing the façade of the Château de Blois toward a branching of rib-faults at the summit.

The staircase was the bravura showpiece of Renaissance architects.[43] It has to be regarded as symbolic rather than functional: climbing to the upper floors was no more important in the sixteenth century than in the Middle Ages. Once again, French architectural tradition was enlarged by an influx of Italian modernism. We have seen the importance in medieval courtyards of the great spiral staircase jutting out from the main building and becoming the chief ornamental feature of the façade (it is almost a caricature of itself at Meillant) or opening out onto tinid loggias, as it does on the top floor of the Château de Nantes. The façade of Chateaudun is illuminating. The two main buildings stand side by side, one dating from the fifteenth and the other from the early sixteenth century, and each has its own staircase, as if the architect of the later building felt bound to compete in this vital area. Both are spiral staircases, but the second is grander, more massively built, with wider openings than the first, and a comparison between them seems to be offered with some satisfaction, as if the staircases were models side by side in an exhibition. The final act, or apotheosis, in this dramatization of the medieval staircase was in the courtyard of the Château de Blois, when the François I staircase was built around 1519. It is a structure sufficient unto itself, still spiral, still jutting from the building, but with many open bays and loaded with ornamentation. Italy introduced two innovations into these developments: the taste for loggias, arcades and galleries, and the straight staircase with turns between its flights.

The fact that the Italianization of French architecture was not just a veneer but a genuine appropriation of foreign forms[44] is illustrated by the many intermediate attempts of French masons to unwind the spiral staircase without sacrificing its grace or its economical surface area. We first find a straight staircase at Josselin, around 1510. It has no landings and turns around an axis at the end of each flight, like the staircase of Chenonceaux built a few years later, with each flight ending in a gallery. At Bonnivet, the projecting staircase was fully integrated with the centre of the façade and was indeed its principal feature, the rest being symmetrically divided on each side of it. The same occurs at Azay-le-Rideau, where the staircase is straight and has wide landings with double openings forming galleries looking out on the courtyard; they are profusely ornamented. In the Loire region, the straight staircase beneath a semi-circular arch with a coffered ceiling was developed further around 1540 at Poncé-sur-le-Loir, and in the nuns' dormitory at Fontevrault Abbey, where it rises in a single flight without any turns; it was later adopted for Henri II's Louvre. The courtyard of the Château d'Ecouen contains a monumental staircase projecting from a wing looking out on the courtyard, with galleries at the landings; it could be described as the adult version of the youthful model found at Bonnivet and Azay-le-Rideau.

In the châteaux of the Loire, the phenomenon of the greatly enlarged staircase reached its apogee at Blois and Chambord. At Chambord, its debt to the quasi-mystical tradition of the monumental staircase, a symbol of the rise of absolute monarchy and to the Italian virtuosity of Leonardo da Vinci are one and same thing[45]; the two concepts are intricately enmeshed. Leonardo set out to design intersecting staircases like pieces of precision engineering. A staircase thus became symbolic of the technology of production just then coming into the ascendant. At Chambord, and indeed in the rest of France

Philibert de l'Orme
Le Premier tome de l'Architecture
The Bad Architect
Paris, 1567

at this period, the two symbols co-existed; like the double spiral of the Chambord staircase, they were intertwined yet separate and though in eyeshot of each other, never met.

Façades thus treated as ends in themselves, provided a perfect site for bas-relief ornamentation.[46] Here again, the proliferation of surface decoration and tendency to fill any empty space with it was typical of late Gothic art. The dormer windows overlooking the courtyard at Josselin and the staircase at Meillant are profusely ornamented with Flamboyant motifs, like the religious architecture of the time. The imposition of rigorous order on the châteaux of the Loire channelled this ornamentation and confined it to certain well-defined areas: door and window frames and their surroundings, lintels, window bases, along cornices (which sometimes assumed huge proportions), for instance at Blois, and balconies, for instance at Amboise. Finally, ornamentation was lavished on the pediments of dormers, on chimneys and on metal finials. We see here the advent of a discipline controlling ornamentation and eschewing the extravagances of Flamboyant art. Here too Italian motifs are juxtaposed or mingled with Gothic motifs. While the new style of architecture itself did not travel particularly well, and could not instantly replace time-honoured building methods or the practical experience of the masons, decorative patterns were easily diffused via engravings, embroidery, fabrics, ceramics, majolica, cabinet-work, jewellery and even printing, which used such motifs in ornamental bands and frontispieces. Quite soon after the Italian campaigns, therefore, motifs in the style of classical antiquity – foliated scrolls, candelabra, arabesques, *putti*, and soon – were being expertly deployed on the portals of churches and châteaux, for instance at Amboise, Gaillon and Bury, and then at Chenonceaux, Azay-le-Rideau and Chambord. The new style also made its way into religious architecture, which in France had a particularly strong ornamental tradition. The porches of the chapel at Ussé and the collegiate churches of Montrésor and Les Roches-Tranchelion are adorned with concave niches, and fleurons imitated from the Charterhouse of Pavia replace the *feuilles de chou* motifs of Flamboyant art.

The most remarkable and significant factor of all is the decoration of the disproportionately large dormer windows on the roofs of fifteenth-century and early sixteenth-century châteaux. It shows a struggle for influence between northern, Flamboyant designs, their curves distorted and broken like German Gothic script, and Italianate forms, rounded and well-balanced like an Aldo Manuzio typeface. French decorators of dormer pediments hesitated for some time between the pointed gable flanked by pinnacles and the curved shell flanked by lanterns, and each invented his own motif, often a compromise between the two. This situation led to the complex, unpredictable designs of curve and counter-curve to be seen at Chenonceaux, Azay-le-Rideau, Ussé and Chambord. The Mediterranean world was steadily gaining ground at this period. Economic and political models were coming from the south, not from Flanders, and France was obliged to turn her back on the Empire for a while. Consequently, the ornamentation of the châteaux of this period is Italianate, taking care to respect the structure of the building itself and clearly emphasizing its functional axes – windows and doors, the position of the floors, the staircase – and there is an increasing disinclination to let ornamental motifs proliferate all over the walls like a tapestry in stone. A number of new motifs appear, illustrating the warlike attributes of a victorious nation. Even at Azay-le-Rideau, which is far from military in style, the ornamental foliage is arranged around chivalric motifs of arrows and quivers, halbards, swords, cuirasses and torches. But the most prominent motif of all, visible from a far and taking pride of place on balconies and pediments, consisted of the initials of the owner's name or his chosen emblem, in the Italian fashion. At Azay-le-Rideau, the G.B. of Gilles Berthelot and the P.L. of Philippe Lesbahy constantly remind us that the château was no longer a place where the court assembled but a private property. In the history of the château, this was something of a revolution.

Philibert de l'Orme
Le Premier tome de l'Architecture
The Good Architect
Paris, 1567

The new organizing principle: Balance

… The pursuit of balance in the design of the façade emphasized stable lines and strong horizontals …

BELOW:
Château du Lude
begun 1457, for Jean de Daillon
South building and angle towers,
built 1520–1530 for Jacques de Daillon

The underlining of form

… The load lines are emphasized to symbolizing order and geometric
mastery of planes and surfaces…

Ornamentation accentuating the structure

… Ornamentation becomes organic, an integral part of the
architectural structures; fantasy is reined in and rationality prevails …

Below:
Château du Lude
South lodging, 1520–1530
Window frame on angle tower

Château de Villegongis
1531–1538, for Jacques de Brizay

Facing Page:
Main building and angle towers
Above Right and Right:
Ornamentation on the façade

Château de Châteaudun

Longueville wing, 1511–1532
Renaissance staircase, 1511–1518
RIGHT:
Corner with the Dunois wing (left),
1459–1469
Gothic staircase, late 15th century

FACING PAGE:
Château de Blois
François I wing, 1515–pre-1524
Staircase, 1519–1520

The importance of the staircase

… The staircase, making much of the absence or presence of turns and
landings, lends drama to the whole façade …

Château de Blois
François I wing, 1515–pre-1524
Staircase, 1519–1520

ABOVE:
Ribbed vault rising from the newel
RIGHT:
Detail of the balustrade of the spiral staircase

FACING PAGE:
Château de Châteaudun
Longueville wing, 1511–1532
Renaissance staircase, 1511–1518
Newel and steps radiating from it

The staircase as motive force

… The staircase animates and energizes the entire building …

Above and Facing Page Below:
Château de Poncé-sur-le-Loir
1525–1535, built for the de Chambray family
Interior of staircase
Flight of steps with barrel vault

The straight staircase

… The spiral staircase did not lend itself to ceremonial processions, and was gradually replaced by the straight staircase. The earliest examples (c. 1510) are found at Josselin and Bonnivet, followed by Azay-le-Rideau and Poncé-sur-le-Loir. It later became the standard in civil architecture of the classical style …

ABOVE AND FACING PAGE BELOW:
Château de Poncé-sur-le-Loir
Interior of staircase
Details of coffering in barrel vault

The staircase as backdrop

… The staircase, prominently placed at the centre of the château, was conceived as a dramatic setting for the master of the house and his guests …

ABOVE AND RIGHT:
Château de Chambord
The keep, 1519–1539
Capitals of the staircase, c. 1530

Above and Facing Page Below:
Château de Chambord
The keep, 1519–1539
Guardroom and double spiral staircases,
invented by Leonardo da Vinci

BELOW:
Leonardo da Vinci
Sketch for a staircase, fortifications and a lantern tower
Pen drawing, between 1516 and 1519

The last outcrop of chivalry: The lantern at Chambord

… The staircase at Chambord becomes an almost mystical structure, resembling a temple or lighthouse; it clearly symbolizes the enlightened and absolute monarchy …

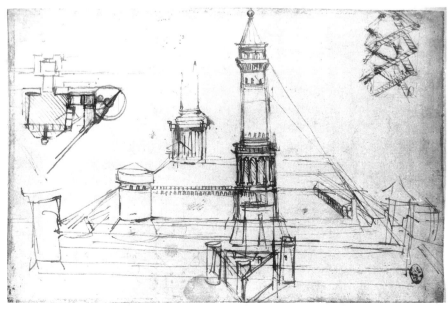

Château de Chambord
The keep, 1519–1539

FACING PAGE ABOVE:
View of the staircase, seen from below

BELOW:
Lantern tower, seen from the terrace

The Charterhouse of Pavia

Church, 1433–1473
Right and Facing Page Above:
Details of façade
architect G. A. Amadeo, 1481–1499
sculptors B. Briosco, C. Lombardo,
early 16th century

The influence of Pavia

… Memories of the Charterhouse of Pavia, much admired by the French during their Italian campaigns, seem to haunt the Château de Chambord; slate is used instead of the black marble of Pavia, and the turrets look like belfries…

BELOW:
Château de Chambord
The keep, 1519–1539
North-west façade

Flamboyant decor

… Culs-de-lampe and capitals appear here and there, like reversions to or survivals of Flamboyant art integrated into the new order of architecture …

Château de Chambord
The keep, west terrace and roof
Ornamentation

<small>ABOVE:</small>
Corner capitals
<small>RIGHT:</small>
Scroll of dormer

Château de Chambord
The keep, west terrace and roof
Ornamentation

Above and Facing Page Below:
Culs-de-lampe

A taste for antiquity

… Shells and foliated designs appear around doors and dormer windows, showing a preference for the antique rather than the Gothic style, for putti and lanterns rather than *feuille de chou* pinnacles …

ABOVE:
Château de Blois
François I wing, 1515–pre-1524
Staircase, 1519–1520
Medallion on the base of the staircase

ABOVE:
Château du Lude
South wing, 1520–1530
Façade of main building: window base

Château d'Ussé
Chapel of the collegiate church, 1523–1535
Detail of doorway

FACING PAGE BELOW:
Ornamentation of the
tympanum
ABOVE AND RIGHT:
Impost capitals

Cornices

… The cornice is a difficult area: at a certain level the architect has to mark the division between earth and sky. The profusely ornamented cornices of the châteaux of the Loire show that there is no clear-cut point of transition …

Château de Valençay
Detail of cornice

ABOVE:
North wing, 1579
LEFT:
Entrance pavilion, between 1540 and 1579

Château de Blois
Detail of cornice

FACING PAGE:
François I wing, 1515–pre-1524
RIGHT:
Louis XII wing, 1498–1504
Detail of cornice

BELOW:
Château d'Azay-le-Rideau
1518–1527
Roof of east façade of right wing

The emblematic function of dormers

… Proudly displayed like a frontispiece to the château, the dormers acted as its owner's emblem, proudly displaying his monogram …

Château de Blois
Louis XII wing, 1498–1504
Roof overlooking the courtyard; dormer
with monogram of Louis XII

ABOVE:
Château de Chambord
The keep, 1519–1539
North-west roof

7

THE NEW MASTERS

The history of the châteaux of the Loire did not end at Pavia. Thousands of tourists flock to see them today, attracted by the world that they evoke. The idea of the fairy-tale castle owes much to them, and we are reminded of them when we visit Pierrefonds or Disneyland. Nostalgia and popular imagination respond less to the châteaux of the Renaissance, altered by modernization and their already ambiguous social status, than to the châteaux of the late fifteenth century with their towers and their battlements, the property of the last great lords, who enjoyed the benefits of peace and luxury without prejudice to their old prerogatives.

This ideal château is frequently to be found on a hillside or standing at the end of an avenue in Touraine or Anjou, bristling with fake machicolations and Gothic ornamentation, and it usually dates from the middle of the nineteenth century. After 1830 – even more noticeably after 1848 – the aristocrats and in particular the legitimists who had held important posts during the Restoration found themselves once again excluded from the political world of Paris. France was enjoying a period of extraordinary economic expansion – as she had under Louis XI – and it enriched them even if they stood by tradition and, unlike the Orléanists, refused to take any part in the new industrial development. Many of them preferred to show their opposition by retiring to their lands, from which they derived a considerable income. There they built châteaux in a reactionary style which spectacularly recalled the last great period of feudalism, as if it had never been interrupted, and the alliance between the kings and the bourgeoisie, the taming of the nobility and finally the triumph of the Third Estate, had been the merest parentheses in the history of France. They chose to return to ancestral tradition at a point where wealth founded solely on land ownership became entangled with finance and trade. Architecture was the means they employed to proclaim their reactionary ambitions and impress them upon the neighbourhood, just as it had been in the sixteenth century. An Angevin architect called René Hodé made this reverse renaissance his speciality, supplying the demands of a new clientèle consisting of right-wing politicians such as Falloux and Mayaud, and noble families enriched by the Restoration such as those of the comte de Quatrebarbes and the marquis de Dreux Brézé. His masterpiece, the Château de Challain-La-Potherie, was built for the largest landowner in the area, François de la Rochefoucauld Boyers, president of the *Conseil Général*.[47]

The architecture of these nineteenth-century châteaux was rudimentary: the simple proportions, particularly on the façades, aimed only at an external effect. Although the interiors sometimes had the advantage of such modern comforts as heating and wallpaper, the general outline of Le Plessis-Bourré, Largeais or Azay-le-Rideau was automatically imitated, sometimes to the point of caricature, and simplified until it became platitudinous. It is not unreasonable to regard the architectural historicism of the nineteenth century as mainly indebted to the late fifteenth-century châteaux of the Loire, but we must qualify this rather sweeping view with reference to the complex position of the French aristocracy in the nineteenth century. A good example in many respects, and a very varied one, is provided by the history of the new nineteenth-century owners of Azay-le-Rideau, the de Biencourt family.[48] The first of them, Charles, Marquis de Biencourt (1747–1824) was prominent among those progressive aristocrats , at the time of the Revolution maintained their royalist views, but accepted and even urged the need for greater justice and democracy, for egalitarian reforms and the abolition of their own privileges. As a deputy from the nobility to the Estates General, this forty-two-year-old soldier, a field-marshal and a Chevalier de Saint-Louis, supported union with the Third Estate and in 1791, like the good citizen he was, complied with the orders of the Assemblée Constituante.

Charles de Biencourt's wife, the daughter of a councillor of state, had brought him a large fortune, which in 1787 allowed him to acquire the Château d'Azay-le-Rideau, on the market at the time for lack of any heirs. He became mayor of Azay-le-Rideau in 1812. Still a convinced royalist, he welcomed the Restoration, and consequently lost the post of mayor during the Hundred Days, although he regained after Waterloo and was mayor until his death in 1824. Azay-le-Rideau therefore underwent the kind of restoration given by the reinvigorated nobility to its châteaux, though this aristocrat was not excessively traditionalist, or he would never have purchased a château built by a financier and bearing the suspect signs of the Italian Renaissance.

Charles de Biencourt's children returned to the fold of legitimist opposition, but without relinquishing the château their father had acquired. His son served in Louis XVI's guard and defended the king at the Tuileries on 10 August. He too became mayor of Azay, inherited the château and undertook its restoration. He describes the way he "hastily made interior arrangements for the sole purpose of rendering the château more suitable for habitation, retaining the pavilion built during his father's long illness and using it as a billiard room and library adjacent to the provisionally repaired salon".[49] A billiard room was as essential to a prosperous household as the keep had once been. He replaced the old keep of Azay-le-Rideau itself, which even the builders of the Renaissance had respected, with "a new tower ... more in

Isidore Deroy
Château de Chenonceaux
Lithograph, 1844

keeping with the attractive Renaissance style", restored the dormers and the barrel vault of the great staircase, along with its *culs-de-lampe* and medallions, which he completed with portraits of the kings of France up to Henri IV. The restoration of the château of Azay was the work of the architect Charles Dussillon in 1845, and it was continued by Armand, Charles de Biencourt's grandson, who was responsible for completing Gilles Berthelot's château by adding a final turret to its north-east corner in 1856. This turret, modelled on its sisters, replaced a ridiculously small Gothic *échauguette* which had been added to the unfinished corner. The château, completed at last, has a harmonious appearance which, though entirely genuine, is felicitous: Armand de Biencourt's good taste deserves acknowledgement.

Armand de Biencourt too had opted for the army, but was so fervent a legitimist that he resigned his commission on the succession of the Orléans monarchy in 1830. He had married the rich heiress of Prince de Montmorency-Tancarville, and was one of the generation of aristocrats who retired to their lands to run their own affairs and live in their renovated châteaux. Armand de Biencourt died in 1862, leaving the château refurbished and full of works of art. His son Charles brought this resurgence of the French nobility full circle, with a typical disaster: he was one of the administrators of the Union Générale, the Catholic and nationalist bank which drained money from the right and extreme right under the Third Republic before failing in a resounding crash in 1882. By the end of that year Azay-le-Rideau was on sale with its furniture and its collections. The ruined administrator saw his fortune swallowed up in attempts to reimburse the creditors of the Union Générale, and he died in 1914, still a member of the right-wing Action Française, in his flat in Paris, where he was writing a work of social history entitled *Les Institutions et règlements de charité aux XVIe et XVIIe siècles*. His wonderful château was too expensive to find a buyer: the nobility had exhausted their credit and the men with new money preferred modern buildings. Azay was finally sold, first in 1899, then again by auction in 1903, and almost immediately, for the third time, in 1904. However, this was the last sale, for the state, as heir to the property of the nobility, acquired it and maintained it from that point on. It was respectfully restored by the Historical Monuments department. The architect Hardion has left us some superb wash drawings of this period, showing the fragile portions that he had to restore: delicate reliefs on the dormers and staircase carved in the friable limestone, work bound to be perishable by the very nature of the material.

The dual noble and bourgeois origins of the châteaux of the Loire continued to mark their history in the nineteenth century. Azay returned to the aristocracy, while its cousin Chenonceaux remained in the hands of financiers. In 1733 Louis-Henri, duke of Bourbon, had ceded it to the *fermier-général* Claude Dupin, a protégé of Louis XIV's great banker Samuel Bernard. His wife, Madame Dupin, made it famous as a place where many illustrious figures were entertained, including Jean-Jacques Rousseau, who stayed there in 1747. In 1864, the rich Madame Pelouze bought Chenonceaux from the descendants of the Dupins, and led an equally luxurious life there. She had the château restored by the architect Félix Roguet between 1865 and 1878.[50] In 1913 Chenonceaux passed into the hands of Gaston Menier of the chocolate-manufacturing firm, and it was used as a hospital during the First World War.

The most edifying story is that of the Château de Chaumont[51], where at the end of the nineteenth century a marriage between aristocracy and finance revived the splendours of a court worthy of the Ancien Régime. The marriage was that of Prince Amédée de Broglie and the young Marie Say, heiress of the sugar billionaire, whose father had given her the château as a present on her sixteenth birthday. This was the fulfilment of the old political dream of an alliance between money and nobility, an idea that both parties had rejected under the monarchy; it was realized only under the Republic, when the nobility no longer had anything to win or lose. Once again the Château de Chaumont experienced the kind of life it had known under the old kings of France: it was entirely restored, refitted, heated, lit and furnished. The village was demolished to extend the park, and rebuilt around a brand-new church on the banks of the Loire. Thanks to the prince's generosity and the Say fortune, Chaumont-sur-Loire was one of the first French villages to have the benefit of running water, electricity (brought there in 1898) and a cinema. The water and electricity served both the villagers and the prince's stables, whose luxury and comfort can still be admired today: forty-two horses and fifteen carriages were kept in upholstered stalls with enamelled mangers and gleaming horse brasses, and the grooms wore white livery bearing the de Broglie arms. A special kitchen made the horses' daily feed. The companies of the Comédie Française and the Opéra came to Chaumont by special train, and the Maharajah of Kapurthala, who had given the de Broglies an elephant, was brought up the river by their private steamboat the *Victoria* when he came to visit them.

The château acquired a more gracious outline when it was remodelled by the architect Jules de La Morandière. It was set in 2,500 hectares of land, with 33 kilometres of access roads, and a number of curious outbuildings made of reinforced concrete. However, the crash of 1929 brought the new dream to an end, just as the failure of the Union Générale had ended the dream at Azay. The de Broglies had to sell Chaumont, and in 1938 the state acquired it.

We may wonder what happened to the royal châteaux under a republic. Their fate reflected the misfortunes of the monarchy, and their history was a wretched one. The options were total ruin, integration with the state and political recovery, or a return to the princely families at the time of the Restoration. Amboise, Blois and Chambord all experienced these vicissitudes, and throughout the nineteenth century they represented a battlefield between

legitimists, moderate republicans and radicals; the entire spectrum of political opinion.

Isidore Deroy
La Loire et ses bords, 1849
Château de Chaumont

Amboise was the least fortunate.[52] When the Empire gave the château to the senator Roger Ducos, that new-made nobleman of the imperial aristocracy discovered "the poor state of several buildings, which are unfit for use, and considerable funds would be required for their restoration, so that to some extent demolition seems advisable". The old fortified castle was in ruins, and the greater part of it was in fact demolished. At the time of the Restoration, in 1815, it passed into the hands of the duchess of Orléans, and then to her son Louis-Philippe. The Second Republic confiscated it and kept the Arab emir Abd el Kader in exile there from 1848 to 1852. The Third Republic, during its early and still monarchist period, returned it to the Orléans family, who still own it.

The buildings of Blois were no better maintained by the declining monarchy.[53] The Regent had sought to exile the Parliament to it, and Louis XVI had ordered its demolition. The château was used to accommodate former royal servants, as a meagre reward, and the unmaintained walls and roofs were threatened by ruin. Proposals were made in 1825 to transfer the prefecture to the château, and in 1875 to make it the town hall. Among all these republican propositions, the Bonapartist idea of ceding it to the Prince Imperial surfaced in 1860. The gift was accepted, but the transfer never came into effect: it is still owned today by the city of Blois, and today houses the municipal library and art museum.

The legacy of Chambord was the most difficult of all to deal with, and considering what it represented its history was archetypal.[54] It too was largely ruined. Two different and highly symbolic proposals for it were made after the Revolution. In 1792, the idea of using it for a free school was put forward; another project was to make it a Quaker colony, an ideal settlement based on democracy and virtue in the American image, instead of the "haunt of vultures" and palace of debauchery the maréchal de Saxe had made of it. The next proposition was for a model village: "We therefore suggest that you order the former Château de Chambord to be entirely razed and demolished, and that the purchaser of materials be commissioned to build fifty houses, each consisting of two rooms, a stable and a barn." Rejecting these liberal proposals, Bonaparte first installed the 15th cohort of the Légion d'Honneur in the château and then, in 1806, gave it to maréchal Berthier. In 1821 a national subscription was launched to restore it to the "miraculous child", the duc de Berry's posthumous son and heir to the throne. At this juncture the corrosive voice of the pamphleteer Paul-Louis Courier of Tours was raised, pointing out the contrast between the virtue of the republicans and the uselessness of the aristocracy: "Twelve thousand acres of enclosed land in Chambord park is a very fine present to give anyone who knows how to cultivate it!"[55]

It is interesting to note that the word "'restoration" has one sense in politics and another in architecture. In the nineteenth century the two senses coincided, and there was much play on the double meaning: to some people restoration meant a return to the Ancien Régime, to others the integration of the monarchist inheritance into a moderate republic. The latter felt much the same about the royal châteaux as had the sixteenth-century financiers who managed to integrate themselves into the feudal system by imitating its architecture. The historicism of the Second Empire, which paid tribute to the Renaissance – just as the Middle Ages were venerated after 1820 – showed how necessary it was to bring together different and even discordant values in a new, politically ecumenical régime: the nation's cultural heritage had to be properly administered too.

The national heritage was another battlefield, one where everyone claimed pre-eminence and sought to assert privileges by citing historical authority. Historical and archaeological theories initially encouraged the historicism of national reconciliation, then gave way to the extreme nationalism of the late nineteenth century and the years before the 1914 war. François Gebelin regards this period as one "of endless controversy over the respective parts played by the French and by foreigners in constructing these buildings".[56] Léon Palustre[57] set himself to defend France. Louis Courajod[58] was a supporter of Italy, while the German art historian Heinrich von Geymüller[59] relegated the French to the rôle of mere craftsmen. In 1910, Marius Vachon gave his book on the French Renaissance the subtitle of *L'Architecture nationale*, calling the first chapter *L'Essor national.*[60] It took the serenity of the post-war period and the intelligence of François Gebelin, writing in 1927, for the debate to emerge from such sterile, partisan scholarship, and it cannot yet be said that the process is complete, or that French theorists have come out of it unscathed.

The people of France and the tourists who visit the valley of the Loire are the legitimate owners of the châteaux today: they come in great crowds, but theirs are peaceful cohorts. Yet enjoyment of this legacy cannot be entirely innocent. It is as well to know *what* has been inherited, *what* is so much admired. What was that power of which the châteaux are the image? What lost world do we seek in them, a world which still casts its spell over us today? What do the châteaux represent in the new politics of national heritage and tourism? Historians of architecture are duty bound not to gloss over these questions, but to offer the visitor the wherewithal to make a critical assessment, the only defence against the magnificent falsehoods these eloquent façades represent.

Feudal nostalgia

Château de Challain-la-Potherie, 1848
architect, René Hodé

FACING PAGE ABOVE RIGHT:
View of the façade as seen from the park
Lithograph by A. Maugendre, c. 1860
ABOVE AND FACING PAGE BELOW:
View from the river running past the park

Château d'Azay-le-Rideau
Restored 1845 onwards
architect, Charles Dussillon

ABOVE:
View from the "English-style" park
RIGHT:
The château before 1845
Lithograph by I. Deroy
FACING PAGE:
View of the north tower replacing the
old keep, 1854

The new owners:
The liberal aristocracy at Azay-le-Rideau

"… His son hastily arranged the interior layout for the sole purpose of rendering the château more suitable for habitation …

He was entirely responsible for the new tower, which replaces the old keep and is in better keeping with the attractive Renaissance style, and for the restoration of the vaults and of the dormers in the original style in which they were built, as well as the restoration of all the ornamentation of the great staircase, where he had the *culs-de-lampe* and medallions which adorn the vault of the staircase carved, adding depictions of the line of kings and queens of France from Louis XI to Henri IV. The dykes and embankments to protect the gardens and the new park from being flooded by the river were also the work of M. the Marquis de Biencourt."

Armand de Biencourt, *Notice sur Azay-le-Rideau,* 1855

The new industrialists at Chenonceaux

"… There is a singularly suave, aristocratic and serene aura about the Château de Chenonceaux. It stands some way from the village, which preserves a respectful distance. You glimpse the château at the end of a great avenue of trees; it is surrounded by woodland and an immense park with fine lawns. Built over the water, it raises its turrets and square chimneys into the air. The Cher passes beneath it, murmuring around the base of its arches as their angled pillars break the current. All is peaceful and gentle, elegant yet robust. It is calm without tedium, melancholy without resentment."

Gustave Flaubert, *Par les champs et les grèves. Touraine et Bretagne,* 1847

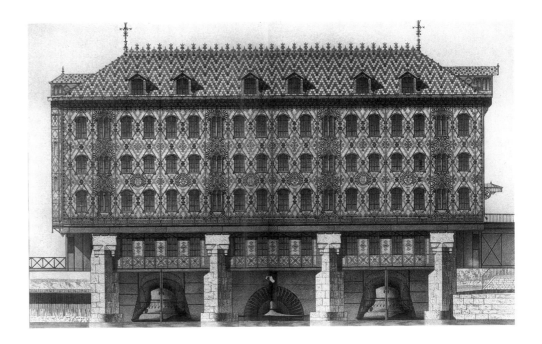

RIGHT:
Noisiel-sur-Marne (Seine-et-Marne)
The Menier factory, 1871–1872
architect, Jules Saulnier
Encyclopédie d'Architecture, 1874

Château de Chenonceaux
The Bohier logis and gallery on the Cher;
restoration begun 1865
architect, Félix Roguet

ABOVE:
East view, from the gardens of Diane
de Poitiers
FACING PAGE BELOW:
West view from the left bank of the Cher

The alliance of aristocracy and finance at Chaumont

"… A simpler building attracts the traveller's attention by virtue of its magnificent position and imposing mass; this is the Château de Chaumont. Built on the loftiest hill along the river banks, its high walls and great towers crown the wide summit. Tall slate-roofed belfries draw the eye to those walls and towers, giving the whole building the monastic air and religious aspect peculiar to all our old châteaux, an air that imparts a serious character to the landscape of most of our provinces. Dark, densely branched trees surround this old manor on all sides, and from a distance resemble the feathers on King Henri's hat; a pretty village stands on the river bank at the foot of the hill, its white houses seeming to spring from the golden sand. It is linked to the château which protects it by a narrow path that winds up through the rock. There is a chapel half-way up the hill; the lords descended and the villagers mounted to worship; it was a place of equality set like a neutral city between poverty and grandeur, which have too often been at war with each other."

Alfred de Vigny, *Cinq-Mars…*, 1826

Château de Chaumont
Restored from 1847
architects, Jules de la Morandière and
Paul-Ernest Sanson

<small>FACING PAGE ABOVE:</small>
Stables, 1878, P.-E. Sanson
<small>FACING PAGE BELOW:</small>
View of the château from the banks of the
Loire
<small>ABOVE:</small>
View from the north, wash drawing
by P.-E. Sanson
<small>LEFT:</small>
Cement bridge in the park, late 19th century

Château de Blois
François I wing, façade of the loggias

The royal residences and the state

"… The Château de Blois. – On its north side the Château de Blois, standing on formidable walls, presents a delightful view of a gallery with a double arcade. Henri III's chamber lay there, with his oratory next to it, a coincidence not unusual in itself but which strikes one forcibly here, in a man whose sensuality was stimulated by religion and whose cruelty was whetted by fear. When we had gone through a winding vaulted passage we entered the interior courtyard of the château. There was much rejoicing there: the garrison had been given a bottle of wine apiece, and the soldiers were carrying jugs full of a blue liquid and preparing to drink the health of the king whose feast-day had brought them this treat."

Gustave Flaubert, *Par les champs et les grèves. Touraine et Bretagne,* 1847

Restoration work

Château de Blois
François I wing, façade of the loggias

Chambord and its park …

"… Four leagues from Blois and a league from the Loire, in a very low-lying little valley among muddy marshes and surrounded by a wood of great oak trees, far from any road, you suddenly come upon a royal or rather a magical château. It looks as if an Oriental djinn, compelled by the power of some wonderful lamp, had snatched it away during one of the Arabian Nights, stealing it from some country of the sun to conceal it in mistier lands, a hiding place for the loves of a handsome prince. This palace is hidden away like buried treasure, but its blue domes and elegant minarets, rounded where they stand on wide walls or rising high into the air, its long terraces looking out over the woods, its slender spires swaying in the wind, its interlacing arches standing all along the colonnades, all this might suggest you were in the realms of Baghdad or Kashmir, were it not for the blackened walls covered with a tapestry of moss and ivy, joining with the pale, melancholy hue of the sky to show that you are in a rainy country."

Alfred de Vigny, *Cinq-Mars…,* 1826

Château de Chambord
completed late 17th century,
gardens laid out and canal built from
the river Cosson, mid-18th century

ABOVE:
South-east view, the Porte Royale side
RIGHT:
Lithograph by Ch. Pensée, 1845
FACING PAGE:
North-west view, the garden side

… an echo of the Absolute

"… Chambord has only one staircase, a double one, so that people going up or down pass each other unseen; everything about it is made for the mysteries of love and war…From a distance, the building is an arabesque, like a woman with her hair blowing in the wind. At closer quarters she becomes part of the masonry and changes into towers; the effect now is of Clorinda propped against ruins. Yet the whimsical impression of a bird in flight has not been dispelled: those delicate, fine-drawn features reappear in the likeness of a dying Amazon. When you go inside you see the fleur-de-lis and salamander on the ceilings. If Chambord were ever destroyed, no record of the pure, early style of the Renaissance would be left anywhere, for in Venice it has been adulterated. Chambord's beauty was restored by its abandonment: through the windows I saw a dried-up flower bed, yellow grass, fields of blackened wheat: marks of the poverty and loyalty of my indigent homeland. While I was there I saw a brown bird of some considerable size flying along the small, unknown river Cosson."

Chateaubriand, *Vie de Rancé*, 1844

Château de Chambord

FACING PAGE:
View of the park
BELOW:
View of the Cosson canal

Map of Châteaux

Historical Overview

Notes

Sources of Quotations

Bibliography

Index

Illustrations

MAP OF CHÂTEAUX

destroyed or in ruins ○
private or closed for restoration ●
open in season ●●
open all the year round ●●●

1. Amboise ●●●
2. Angers ●●●
3. Argy ●●
4. Azay-le-Rideau ●●
5. Baugé (manoir) ●●
6. Beauregard ●●
7. Blois ●●●
8. Bonnivet ○
9. Bury ○
10 Challain-la-Potherie ●
11. Chambord ●●●
12. Châteaudun ●●●
13. Chaumont ●●●
14. Chenonceaux ●●●
15. Cheverny ●●●
16. Chinon ●●●
17. Le Coudray-Montpensier ●
18. Fougères-sur-Bièvre ●●●
19. Le Gué-Péan ●●●
20. Herbault-en-Sologne ●
21. L'Islette ●
22. Langeais ●●●
23. Launay (manoir) ●
24. Lavardin ●●
25. Loches ●●●
26. Le Lude ●●
27. Mehun-sur-Yèvre ○
28. Meillant ●●
29. La Ménitré (manoir) ●
30 Montbazon ●
31. Montpoupon ●●
32. Montrésor ●●
33. Montrichard ●●
34. Mortier-Crolles ●●
35. Le Moulin ●●
36. Le Plessis-Bourré ●●
37. Le Plessis-lès-Tours ●●
38. Poncé-sur-le-Loir ●●
39. Les Réaux ●●●
40 Les Roches-Tranchelion ○
41. Romorantin ○
42. Saumur ●●●
43. Semblançay ○
44. Talcy ●●●
45. Ussé ●●
46. Valençay ●●
47. Le Verger ○
48. Veuil ○
49. Villandry ●●
50. Villegongis ●●
51. Villesavin ●●

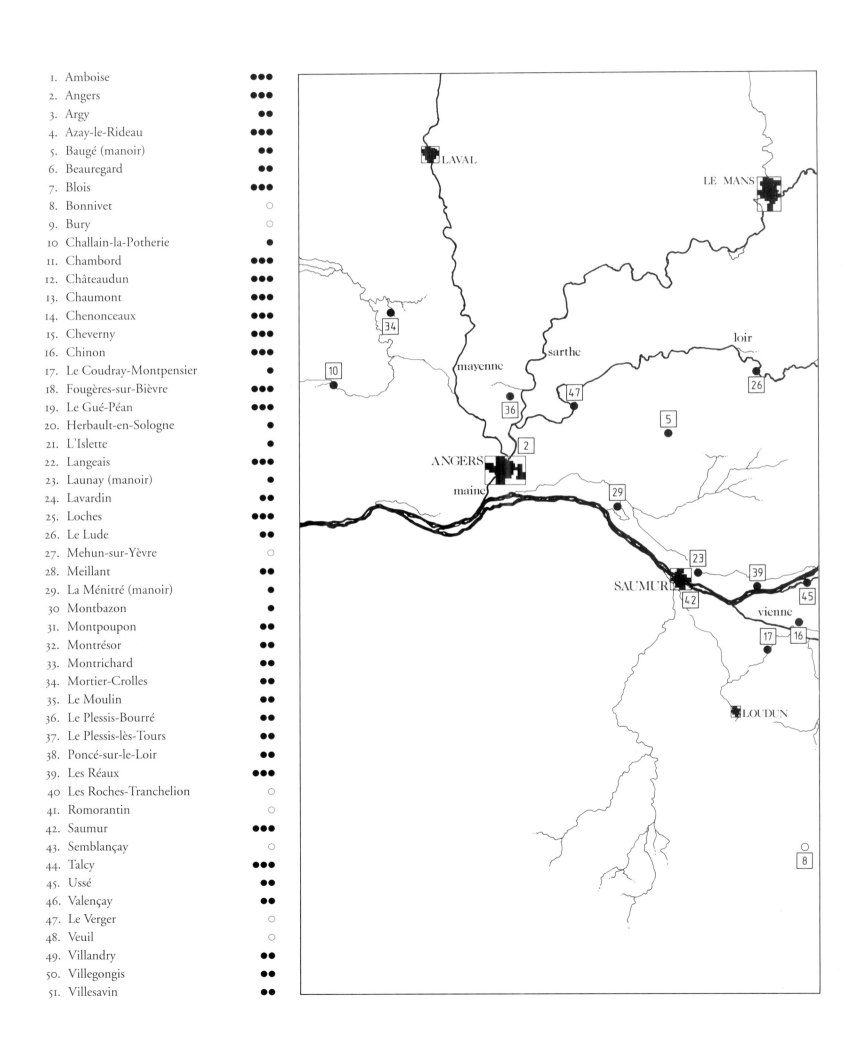

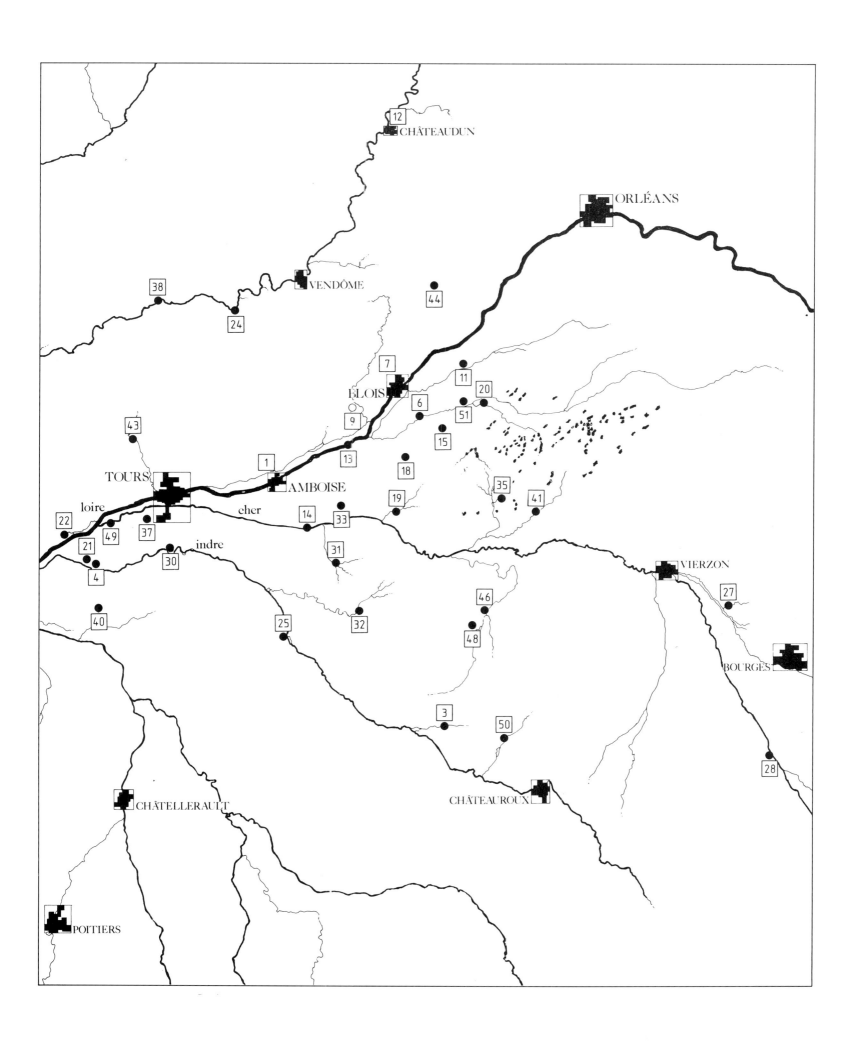

CHÂTEAUDUN

12

ORLÉANS

38

VENDÔME

44

24

7

11

BLOIS

20

6

9

51

43

15

TOURS

1

13

AMBOISE

18

loire

35

19

41

cher

22

14

33

49

21

37

31

VIERZON

indre

30

27

4

46

40

25

32

48

BOURGES

3

50

28

CHÂTELLERAULT

CHÂTEAUROUX

POITIERS

Historical Overview

1337–1453 Hundred-year war

Struggle for the French Crown between England and France. After the French king had suffered heavy defeats and at the same time had to deal with internal conflicts, England was accorded the whole of South West France in the Treaty of Bretigny in 1360.

1380–1422 Reign of Charles VI

1415 The English king Henry V reinstigated the war, forming an alliance with Duke John of Burgundy.

In the Treaty of Troyes in 1420 the marriage of Henry V to Catherine, the daughter of Charles VI, was sealed, confirming the claim of the English king to the throne. The whole of France was then ruled by England and Burgundy, with the exception of Anjou, the Touraine and Orléans.

1422 Death of Henry V.

1422–1461 Reign of Charles VII

1427 Charles VII held court in Chinon.

1429 Joan of Arc freed France from the English. When Charles had regained control of the whole of Orléanias by June 18th, he crowned himself King Charles VII on July 17th in Rheims.

1436 Charles VII was able to win back Paris.

1453 The war ended without an official declaration of peace. The English king had lost all possessions on the Continent to the French king, with the exception of Calais.

1461–1483 Reign of Louis XI

1476 Guerre folle: Revolt of the feudal lords lead by Louis of Orléans.

1481 The Duchy of Anjou reverted to the Crown after the death of King René when its period of feudal tenure ended.

1483–1498 Reign of Charles VIII

1491 Charles VIII married Ann de Bretagne, the heiress of Brittany.

1494–1559 Italian campaigns

of the French kings Charles VIII, Louis XII and Francis I in order to assert their claims on the heritage on the House of Anjou, the kingdom of Naples and the Eastern Roman imperial crown. The rulers were confronted with a completely different culture and way of life, which they became enthusiastic about and attempted to imitate.

1492 Charles VIII began working on the Chateau d'Amboise.

1498–1515 Reign of Louis XII

When Charles VIII died childless, Louis of Orléans, a great-nephew of Charles VI, became his heir. In order to ensure that Brittany remained bound to France he had to marry Ann de Bretagne first, however.

1514 Their daughter, Claude de France, was married to Francis d'Angoulême, the future Francis I.

1498 Louis XII began renovation of the old Chateau de Blois.

1515–1547 Reign of Francis I

Francis I promoted the arts and brought Italian artists to his court; in 1516, Leonardo da Vinci came to France. During his period of rule an immense number of building projects were initiated. In 1525 he was defeated in the Battle of Pavia by his rival for the imperial crown, Charles V of Spain and spent a year in imprisonment. After his return in 1528, he decided to live in Paris, which became his preferred residence.

1547–1559 Reign of Henry II

Henry II was married to Catherine de Medici for political reasons but his mistress, Diana de Poitiers, for whom he made extensive additions to the Chateau de Chenonceaux, was always at his side.

1562–1598 Religious wars

Conflict between the Protestant Huguenots and the Royalist Catholics.

1559–1589 Reign of the three sons of Henry II

Francis II (1559–1560), Charles IX (1560–1574) and Henry III (1574–1589).

The death of Henry III signified the end of the House of Valois.

The Bourbons (1589–1792)

The Era of the Bourbons was the period of absolute monarchy that only came to an end in the 18th century after the Enlightenment and the Revolution. Its Baroque, Rococo and Classicist art left hardly any traces in the Chateaux of the Loire.

Notes

1. Paul Chaussard, *La Marine de Loire*, Roanne 1980.

2. *Ordonnances des rois de France, règne de François Ier*, Vol. II, p. 78, no. 119 (letters of May 1517, quoted by Roger Dion, *Le Val de Loire, étude de géographie régionale*, Tours 1934 (reprinted Marseille 1978).

3. Strabo, *Geographia*, Book IV, quoted by Roger Dion, op. cit.

4. Carlo Pedretti, *Leonardo da Vinci, the Royal Palace at Romorantin*, Cambridge (Mass.) 1972.

5. Arch. Dép. d'Indre-et-Loire, Fonds d'Azay-le-Rideau, E. 980 (for accounts dealing with stone from the quarries, see fol. 8 v° ff.).
On these subjects, see also an article by Jacqueline Melet-Sanson, "Provenance des matériaux utilisés pour la construction des édifices publics de la ville d'Amboise aux XVe et XVIe siècles", in *98e Congrès national des Sociétés savantes*, St-Etienne 1973, archaeological section.

6. Quoted in Claude Launay, *Quand les rois de France étaient en Val de Loire*, Paris 1978.

7. Roger Dion, op. cit.

8. Roger Dion, op. cit., Book II, "Les levées de la Loire".

9. Laurence Berluchon, *Jardins de Touraine*, Tours 1940.

10. Abbé Casimir Chevalier, "La ville d'Azay-le-Rideau au XVe et au XVIe siècle", in *Bulletin archéologique de Touraine*, Vol. II (1873).

11. Ibid.

12. Charles Loyseau, *Traité des Seigneuries*, Book IV, Ch. 25: "On justice", Paris 1608.

13. Louis Hautecoeur, *Histoire de l'architecture classique en France*, Vol. I: La formation de l'idéal classique: Part 1, La première Renaissance, Paris 1963.

14. Jules Maurice, *Azay-le-Rideau et sa région à travers l'histoire*, Tours 1946.

15. Abbé Casimir Chevalier, op. cit.

16. Quoted by Jules Maurice, op. cit.

17. Michel Melot and Jacqueline Melet-Sanson, *Le Château de Chaumont*, Paris 1980.

18. On this subject cf. Michel Melot, "Politique et architecture, essai sur Blois et le Blésois sous Louis XII", in *Gazette des Beaux-Arts*, December (1967).

19. Machiavelli, *Il Principe*, 1512, published 1531. Ch. XX, "Are fortresses, and the many other things to which princes often resort, advantageous or hurtful?"

20. Claude de Seyssel, *La Grande Monarchie de France*, Paris 1519; Claude de Seyssel, *Histoire singulière du roy Louys douziesme ...*, Paris 1558; Charles de Grassaille, *Regalium Franciae Libri duo ...*, Lyon 1538.

21. Accounts of the archduke's reception are to be found in the works of Jean d'Auton and Claude de Seyssel. A particularly detailed description is given in Théodore Godefroy's *Ceremonial françois*, edited by Denys Godefroy, Paris 1649, Vol. II.

22. These details may be found in the *Comptes des menus plaisirs du roi Louis XII*, in the Bibliothèque Nationale, particularly Mss. fr. 2926 and 2927 (for the years 1503–1504).

23. Le Roux de Lincy, *Détails sur la vie privée d'Anne de Bretagne*, in *Bibliothèque de l'Ecole de Chartes*, Vol. XI (1849).

24. Fleuranges (Robert de la Marck), *Mémoires*, in *Choix de chroniques et mémoires sur l'histoire de France ...*, by J.A.C. Buchon, Paris 1836, Vol. XIII.

25. Michel Melot, "Blois au XVIe siècle", in *Blois, la ville, les hommes*, Blois 1974.

26. Useful works to consult on the subject of Leonardo da Vinci's part in the conception of Chambord are: Jean Guillaume, "Léonard de Vinci et l'architecture française: le problème de Chambord", in *Revue de l'Art* (1974), No. 25; Ludwig Heinrich Heydenreich, "Leonardo da Vinci, Architect of Francis I", in the *Burlington Magazine*, Vol. 94 (October 1952); and Carlo Pedretti, *A Chronology of Leonardo da Vinci's Architectural Studies after 1500*, Geneva 1962. Finally, see Jean Guillaume, "Léonard et l'architecture", in *Léonard de Vinci, ingénieur et architecte*, Montreal, 1987.

27. Bernard Chevalier, *Tours, ville royale, 1356–1520*, Paris-Louvain 1975.

28. Georges Bricard, *Un serviteur et compère de Louis XI, Jean Bourré, seigneur du Plessis, 1424–1506*, Paris 1893.

29. Ibid.

30. Bernard Chevalier, op. cit.

31. Jean d'Auton, *Chroniques de Louis XII*, ed. De Maulde, 1889, Vol. IV.

32. Quoted in Alfred Spont, *Semblançay, la bourgeoisie financière au début du XVIe siècle*, Paris 1895.

33. Paul Vitry, *Tours et les châteaux de Touraine*, in *Les Villes d'Art célèbres* series, Paris 1912.

34. Jules Loiseleur, "Etude sur Gilles Berthelot constructer d'Azay-le-Rideau et sur l'administration des finances de son époque", in *Mémoires de la Société Archéologique de Touraine*, Vol. XI (1859).

35. Departmental archives of Indre-et-Loire, series E, Fonds d'Azay-le-Rideau, E. 977, Vol. 7 ff. *Frais avant l'achat définitif d'Azay ...*

36. Departmental archives of Indre-et-Loire, series E, Fonds d'Azay-le-Rideau, E. 979, 27 ff. and E. 980, 39 ff.

37. Jean Guillaume, "Azay-le-Rideau et l'architecture française de la Renaissance", in *Les monuments historiques de la France*, 1976, no. 5.

38. Ibid.

39. Jean Guillaume, "Chenonceaux avant la construction de la galerie. Le château de Thomas Bohier et sa place dans l'architecture de la Renaissance", in *Gazette des Beaux-Arts*, January (1969).

40. On the subject of the initial plan for Chambord, cf. Jean Martin-Demezil, "Chambord", in *Congrès Archéologique de France, 1981*, Paris 1986, p. 20: "There are a number of reasons to suggest that the 'magnificent building' entrusted to the Pontbriand team in 1519 consisted of the 'keep' and the keep alone."

41. Jean Guillaume, "Le Gué-Péan", in *Congrès Archéologique de France, 1981*, Paris 1986.

42. Cf. Jean Guillaume, in *Le Château en France*, a work by several authors, edited by Pierre Babelon, Paris 1986.

43. On this subject, cf. *L'escalier dans l'architecture de la Renaissance, Colloque du Centre d'Études de la Renaissance*, Tours 1979, published in Paris 1985.

44. This is the hypothesis supported by Jean Guillaume, in his chapter on the early Renaissance (1495–1525) in the collective work *Le Château en France*, ed. Pierre Babelon, Paris 1986.

45. Cf. note 27.

46. Jean Guillaume, "L'Ornement italien en France, position du problème et méthode d'analyse", in *La scultura decorativa del primo Rinascimento*, Pavia 1983 (proceedings of the colloquium of 1980).

47. Christian Derouet, "Architecture d'hier: grandes demeures angevines au XIXᵉ siècle. L'Œuvre de René Hodé entre 1840 et 1870", in *Les Monuments historiques de la France*, 1976, no. 4.

48. Pierre Leveel, "Les Biencourt d'Azay", in *Bulletin de la Société Archéologique de Touraine*, Vol. XXXVII (1974).

49. Armand de Biencourt, *Notice sur Azay-le-Rideau*, requested for the work on Touraine edited by M. Mame, departmental archives of Indre-et-Loire, E. 1040, quoted by Pierre Leveel, op. cit.

50. Abbé Casimir Chevalier, *La Restauration du Château de Chenonceaux, 1864–1878*, Lyon 1878.

51. Jacques de Broglie, *Histoire du Château de Chaumont (980–1943)*, Paris 1944.

52. Pierre de Vaissière, *Le Château d'Amboise*, Paris 1935.

53. Frédéric and Pierre Lesueur, *Le Château de Blois, notice historique et archéologique*, Paris 1921, Ch. VI, "L'Abandon".

54. Jean Martin-Demezil, "Chambord", in *Congrès Archéologique de France, 1981*, Paris, Société Française d'Archéologie, 1986.

55. Paul-Louis Courier, *Simple discours de Paul-Louis, vigneron de la Chavonnière ... pour l'acquisition de Chambord*, 1821.

56. François Gebelin, *Les Châteaux de la Renaissance*, Paris 1927.

57. Léon Palustre, *L'Architecture de la Renaissance*, Paris 1892.

58. Louis Courajod, *Leçons professées à l'Ecole du Louvre*, publ. H. Lemonnier and A. Michel, Vol. II, "Origines de la Renaissance", Paris 1899–1903, 3 volumes.

59. Heinrich von Geymüller, *Die Baukunst der Renaissance in Frankreich*, Stuttgart 1898–1901, 2 volumes.

60. Marius Vachon, *La Renaissance française, l'architecture nationale, les grands maîtres maçons*, Paris 1910.

Sources of Quotations

Chapter I

Charles d'Orléans (1394–1465), *Poésies*,
ed. J.-M. Guichard, 1843 (p. 10).

Stendhal, *Mémoires d'un touriste*, 1838 (p. 12).

Pierre de Ronsard, *Le Voyage de Tours*, in *Les Amours*,
Book II, 1553 (p. 15).

Honoré de Balzac, *Le Lys dans la Vallée*, 1839 (p. 16).

Andrea Navagero, *Voyage d'André Navagero en Espagne
et en France*, 1528, in *Relations des Ambassadeurs vénitiens
sur les affaires de France*, 1838 (p. 18).

Pierre de Ronsard, *Elégie sur la forêt de Gastine*, 1584
(p. 20).

Victor Hugo, *En Voyage, Alpes et Pyrénées*, 1843, first
published in the *Œuvres inédites de Victor Hugo*, Hetzel,
1890, Vol. VI (p. 22).

Joachim du Bellay, *Les Regrets*, 1558 (p. 24).

Eugène Viollet-Le-Duc, *Entretiens sur l'architecture*,
eleventh conversation, 1872 (p. 27).

Jérôme Lippomano, *Voyage de Jérôme Lippomano*, 1577,
in *Relations des Ambassadeurs vénitiens sur les affaires de
France*, 1838, Vol. II (p. 31).

Alfred de Vigny, *Cinq-Mars, ou une conjuration sous
Louis XIII*, 1826 (p. 33).

Chapter III

Relation d'une visite du Duc de Bretagne au Roi René,
manuscript in the Archives Nationales P 1334, fol. 223
v°, in Albert Lecoy de la Marche, *Le Roi René, sa vie,
son administration, ses travaux artistiques et littéraires ...*,
1875, Vol. 2 (p. 60).

Philippe de Commynes, *Mémoires*, Book VI, 1498,
edition of the Société de l'Histoire de France,
1840–1847, Vol. II (p. 63).

Jean d'Auton, *Chroniques*, 1502, in Paul L. Jacob,
*Chroniques publiées d'après le manuscrit de la bibliothèque
du roi ...*, 1834, Vol. II (p. 64).

Philippe de Commynes, *Mémoires*, Book VIII, 1498,
in op. cit. (p. 66).

Jean d'Auton, *Chroniques*, 1502, in op. cit., Vol. II
(p. 69).

Jean d'Auton, *Chroniques*, 1506, in op. cit., Vol. III
(p. 70).

Brantôme, *Vie des Dames illustres*, Part One, *Discours
sur la Reyne Anne de Bretagne*, in Ludovic Lalanne,
*Œuvres complètes de Pierre de Bourdeilles, seigneur de
Brantôme*, 1867, Vol. VII (p. 76)

Charles VIII, *Lettre de Naples*, dated 28 March 1495, in
P. Pelicier, *Lettres de Charles VIII*, 1903, Vol. IV (p. 81).

Andrea Navagero, *Voyage d'André Navagero en Espagne
et en France*, 1528, in op. cit. (p. 83).

Brantôme, *Vie des Hommes illustres et des Grands
Capitaines français*, in op. cit., Vol. III, (p. 85).

Chapter VII

Armand de Biencourt, *Notice sur Azay-le-Rideau*,
requested by M. de Sourdeval for publication in
La Touraine, 1855, departmental archives of Indre-et-
Loire, E 1040 (p. 169).

Gustave Flaubert, *Par les champs et les grèves,
Touraine et Bretagne*, 1847 (pp. 170 and 175).

Alfred de Vigny, *Cinq-Mars, ou une conjuration sous
Louis XIII*, 1826 (pp. 172 and 178).

Chateaubriand, *Vie de Rancé*, Book II, 1844 (p. 180).

Bibliography

General Works

Châteaux of the Loire

Le Château en France, ed. Jean-Pierre Babelon, Paris 1986, particularly the chapter by Jean Guillaume on the early Renaissance 1495–1525.

Blunt Anthony, *Art and Architecture in France, 1500–1700,* London 1953 (trad. fr., Paris 1983).

Gebelin François, *Les Châteaux de la Renaissance,* Paris 1927.
  Les Châteaux de la Loire, Paris 1957.

Hautecoeur Louis, *Histoire de l'architecture classique en France,* Vol. I, section one: La première Renaissance, Paris 1963.

Jeanson Denis, *La Maison seigneuriale du Val de Loire,* Paris 1981.

Prinz W. and Kecks R. G. *Das französische Schloß der Renaissance, Form und Bedeutung der Architektur,* Berlin 1985.

The Loire Valley

Babonaux Yves, *Villes et régions de la Loire moyenne, Touraine, Blésois, Orléanais, fondements et perspectives géographiques,* Paris 1966.

Chevalier Bernard, *Tours, ville royale, 1356–1520,* publications of the Sorbonne, Paris–Louvain 1975.

Dion Roger, *Le Val de Loire, étude de géographie régionale,* Tours 1934 (reissued Marseille 1978).

Pérouse de Montclos Jean-Marie, *Architectures en Région Centre, Val de Loire, Beauce, Sologne, Berry, Touraine,* Le Guide du Patrimoine, Paris 1988.

Daily Life

Berluchon Laurence, *Jardins de Touraine,* Tours 1940.

Cloulas Ivan, *La vie quotidienne dans les châteaux de la Loire au temps de la Renaissance,* Paris 1983.

Launay Claude, *Quand les rois de France étaient en Val de Loire,* Paris 1978.

Lefranc Abel, *La vie quotidienne au temps de la Renaissance,* Paris 1938.

Rain Pierre, *Les Chroniques des Châteaux de la Loire,* Paris 1921.

Tourist Guides

Guide du Val de Loire mystérieux, Les Guides noirs, Paris 1968.

Bournon Fernand, *Blois, Chambord et les Châteaux du Blésois,* Paris 1908.

Briais Bernard, *La Vallée de l'Indre,* Tours 1980.

Debraye Henry, *En Touraine et sur les bords de la Loire,* Grenoble 1929.

Guerlin Henri, *La Touraine …,* Paris 1945.

Lanoux Armand, *Itinéraire Paris-Val de Loire,* Paris 1950.

Ranjard R., *La Touraine archéologique, guide du touriste en Indre-et-Loire,* Tours 1930 (ninth edition, Mayenne 1986).

Terrasse Charles, *L'art des châteaux de la Loire,* Paris 1927.

Vitry Paul, *Tours et les châteaux de Touraine,* Paris 1912.

Monographs

Abbrevations

C. A.: Congrès archéologiques de France, published by the Société française d'archéologie
  1925: 88th meeting, held at Blois.
  1931: 94th meeting, held at Bourges.
  1949: 106th meeting, held at Tours.
  1964: 122th meeting, Anjou.
  1981: 179th meeting, Blésois and Vendômois.

P. M.: Series of Petites Monographies on the great buildings of France, ed. Laurens (subsequently Lanore), Paris.

Gebelin: François Gebelin, *Les Châteaux de la Renaissance,* Paris 1927.

Amboise

Gebelin, pp. 37–39.

Vaissière Pierre (de), *Le Château d'Amboise,* Paris 1925.

Azay-le-Rideau

P. M., Henri Guerlin, *Les Châteaux de Touraine…,* 1922.

C. A., 1949, pp. 278–301, by Pierre-Marie Auzas.

Gebelin, pp. 51–53

Guillaume Jean, *Azay-le-Rideau et l'architecture française de la Renaissance in Les Monuments historiques de la France,* 1976, no 5.

Leveel Pierre, *Azay-le-Rideau,* Guides Morancé, Bellegarde n.d.

Maurice Jules, *Azay-le-Rideau et sa région à travers l'histoire,* Tours 1971.

Blois

C. A. 1925, p. 9–189 by Dr Frédéric Lesueur.

Gebelin, pp. 55–56.

Lesueur Frédéric and Pierre, *Le Château de Blois, notice historique et archéologique,* Paris 1914–1921.

Lesueur Frédéric Dr, *Le Château de Blois,* Paris 1970.

Bury

Gebelin, pp. 65–67.

Garczynska-Tissier de Mallerais Martine, *Le Château de Bury, dans information d'histoire de l'art,* 1965.

Chambord

Gebelin, pp. 68–74.

C. A. 1925, pp. 487–494, by Paul Vitry.

P. M. 1931, by Henri Guerlin.

Guillaume Jean, *Léonard de Vinci et l'architecture française: le problème de Chambord,* in *Revue de l'Art,* 1974, No 25.

Prinz W., *Schloß Chambord und die Villa Rotonda in Vincenza,* Berlin 1980.

C. A. 1981, pp. 1–115 by Jean Martin-Demezil.

Metternich Wolfgang, *Schloß Chambord an der Loire – Der Bau von 1517–1524,* Darmstadt 1985.

Châteaudun

Martin-Demezil-Chatenet Monique, *Le Château de Châteaudun,* in *Information d'histoire de l'art,* 1970.

Nicot Guy, *Le Château de Châteaudun,* in *Les Monuments historiques de la France,* 1977, No 5.

Chaumont

C. A. 1925, pp. 454–469 by Dr Frédéric Lesueur.

Bosseboef Louis, *Le Château de Chaumont dans l'histoire et les arts,* Tours 1906.

Broglie Jacques de, *Histoire du Château de Chaumont,* Paris 1944.

Melot Michel and Melet-Sanson Jacqueline, *Le Château de Chaumont,* Paris 1980.

Chenonceaux

C. A., 1949, pp. 226–230 by Marcel Aubert.

P. M. 1928, by Charles Terrasse.

Gebelin, pp. 81–86.

Chevalier Casimir, *Histoire de Chenonceaux,* Lyon 1868.

Le Château de Chenonceaux, Tours 1882.

Guillaume Jean, *Chenonceaux avant la construction de la Galerie, le château de Thomas Bohier et sa place dans l'architecture de la Renaissance, dans Gazette des Beaux-Arts,* January 1969.

Chinon

C. A. 1949, pp. 343–363 by René Crozet.

P. M. 1963, by Eugène Pepin.

L'Islette

Gebelin, pp. 144–145.

C. A., 1949, pp. 273–277 by Pierre-Marie Auzas.

Fougères-sur-Bièvre

C. A. 1925, pp. 470–479, by Marcel Aubert.

C. A. 1981, pp. 197–201, by Monique Chatenet.

Gaillon

Chirol, *Un premier foyer de la Renaissance, le château de Gaillon,* Paris 1952.

Weiss Roberto, *The Castle of Gaillon in 1500–1510,* in *Journal of the Warburg and Courtauld Institutes,* 1953.

Le Gué-Péan

C. A. 1981, pp. 244–258, in Jean Guillaume.

Josselin

P. M., 1954, by Roger Grand.

Langeais

C. A. 1949, pp. 378–400 by Dr Frédéric Lesueur.

P. M. 1922, by Henri Guerlin (Les châteaux de Touraine, Luynes, Langeais, Ussé, Azay).

Loches

C. A. 1949, pp. 111–125, by Jean Vallery-Radot.

P. M. 1954, by Jean Vallery-Radot.

Luynes

P. M. 1922 by Henri Guerlin (Les châteaux de Touraine, Luynes, Langeais, Ussé, Azay).

La Morinière

C. A. 1981, pp. 299–302, by Annie Cosperec.

Le Moulin

C. A. 1925, pp. 190–202, by Marcel Aubert.

Nantes

Dere Anne-Claire, *Anne de Bretagne et son château de Nantes,* in *Bulletin de la Société archéologique et historique de Nantes et de Loire-Atlantique,* No. 119, 1983.

Romorantin

Pedretti, *Leonardo da Vinci, the Royal Palace at Romorantin,* Cambridge, Mass. 1972.

Guillaume Jean, *Léonard de Vinci et l'architecture française: la villa de Charles d'Amboise et le château de Romorantin,* in *Revue de l'Art,* 1974, No 25.

Saint-Aignan-sur-Cher

Gebelin, pp. 160–161.

C. A. 1981, pp. 337–355, by Françoise Boudon.

Talcy

C. A. 1925, pp. 495–508, by Dr Frédéric Lesueur.

Ussé

Gebelin, pp. 172–173.

C. A. 1949, pp. 326–341, by Jean Vallery-Radot.

P. M. 1922, by Henri Guerlin (Les Châteaux de Touraine: Luynes, Langeais, Ussé, Azay).

Valençay

Gebelin, pp. 176.

P. M. 1930, by René Crozet.

Villegongis

Gebelin, pp. 180.

Biographies

Jacques de Beaune de Semblançay

Spont Alfred, *Semblançay, la bourgeoisie financière au début du XVIe siècle...*, Paris 1895.

Jean Bourré

Bricard Georges, *Jean Bourré, seigneur du Plessis*, Paris 1893.

Jacques Coeur

Poulain Claude, *Jacques Coeur ou les rôves concrétisés*, Paris 1982.

René of Anjou

Lecoy de la Marche Albert, *Le Roi René, sa vie, son administration, ses travaux artistiques et littéraires*, 2 vols, Paris 1875.

Levron Jacques, *Le bon Roi René*, Paris 1973.

Louis XI

Kendall Paul Murray, *Louis XI ... "the universal pider"...*, Paris 1974.

Louis XII

Quilliet Bernard, *Louis XII*, Paris 1986.

Thibaut Pascale, *Louis XII: images d'un roi ...*, catalogue d'exposition, Château de Blois, 1987–1988.

François I

Guerdan René, *François Ier, le roi de la Renaissance*, Paris 1976.

Hackett Francis, *François Ier*, Paris 1937.

Jacquart Jean, *François Ier*, Paris 1981.

Lecoq Anne-Marie, *François Ier, imaginaire, symbolique et politique à l'aube de la Renaissance française*, Paris 1987.

Anne of Bretagne

Leroux de Lincy, *Vie de la Reine Anne de Bretagne ...*, Paris 1860, 4 vols.

Markale Jean, *Anne de Bretagne*, Paris 1980.

Index

A

Abd el Kader (1807–1883), Arab emir 164
Action Française 163
Alamand, family 87
Alps 64
Amadeo, Giovanni Antonio (1447–1522) 150
Amasse, river 7
Amboise (Indre-et-Loire) 7, 11, 19, 91
   Clos-Lucé (le) manor of, (manor of Le Cloux until the
    17th century) 19
Amboise, château d' 9, 36, 56, 58–59, 66–67, 72–73,
   77, 80–81, 90, 129, 133, 164
   Chapelle Saint-Hubert 77
   Tour des Minimes 72–73
Amboise, family d'
   Hugues I 43
   Pierre, father of Charles d'Amboise 13, 46
   Georges (1460–1510), archbishop of Rouen and
    cardinal 57–59, 64, 90
   Charles II (d. 1511), nephew of Georges
    d'Amboise 51, 90, 130
America 7
Ancien Régime 163, 165
Angers (Maine-et-Loire) 7–8, 56, 106
Angers, château d' 36, 56
Angoulême, François comte d' (see François I)
Anjou 15, 24, 55, 87, 90–91, 161
Anjou, Louis d' (see Louis I)
   René d' (see René I)
Anne de Bretagne (1477–1514), wife of Charles
   VIII, and then of Louis XII 57–58, 76
Argy, château d' (Indre) 90, 95
Arno, river 12
Arrou, river 7
Artannes (Indre-et-Loire) 16
Artault, Guillaume, abbé de Saint-Cyr 106–107
Atlantic 7
Auton, Jean d' (1466–1527) 90
   Chroniques, 1502 64, 69–70
Avignon 87
Azay-sur-l'Indre (Indre-et-Loire) 36, 38, 90, 105, 107,
   162
Azay-le-Rideau, château d' 7–8, 25, 36–39, 58–59, 87,
   90, 105–109, 111–112, 115, 117–118, 120, 123–124, 126,
   129–130, 132–133, 145, 158, 161–164, 168

B

Babou de la Bourdaisière, family 62
Baghdad 178
Ballan (Indre-et-Loire) 16
Balzac, Honoré de (1799–1850)
   Le Lys dans la Vallée, 1839 16
Bastarnay, Imbert de, seigneur de Bridoré 30
Baugé, manor of (Maine-et-Loire) 56, 61
Bayard, Pierre Terrail, seigneur de (d. 1524) 107
Beauce 81
Beaufort-en-Vallée (Maine-et-Loire) 60

Beaugency (Loiret) 8, 91, 102
Beaujeu, family de 56
   Pierre II, duc de Bourbon, sire de (1430–1503) 63
Beaune, family de 88, 105
   Jacques de, seigneur de Semblançay (1445–1527) 44,
    87–88, 91, 99, 105, 107–108
   Guillaume 90
Beauregard, château de (Loir-et-Cher) 59, 91, 130
Bellay, Joachim du (1522–1560)
   Les Regrets, 1558 24
Bernard, Samuel, comte de Coubert (1631–1739) 163
Berry 9
Berry, Charles Ferdinand de Bourbon, duc de 165
   Jean de France, duc de (1340–1416) 36–37
Berthelot, family 88, 90–91, 105–106
   Jean, father of Martin Berthelot 105
   Martin, father of Gilles Berthelot 90, 105
   Gilenne (Ruzé), aunt of Gilles Berthelot 105
   Jeanne (Briçonnet), aunt of Gilles Berthelot 105
   Marie (Fumée), aunt of Gilles Berthelot 105
   Gilles (d. 1529) 25, 38, 87, 89, 105–108, 111, 133, 162
Berthier, Louis Alexandre (1753–1815), prince of
   Neuchâtel and Wagram, maréchal de France 165
Bèze, Théodore de (1519–1605) 38
Biencourt, family de 162
   Charles de (1747–1824), father of Antoine Marie de
    162
   Antoine Marie de (d. 1854), father of Armand de 169
   Armand de (d. 1862), father of Charles II de 162–163,
    169
   Charles II de 163
Blois (Loir-et-Cher) 7–10, 18, 22, 37–39, 56–59, 70,
   76, 83, 91, 97–98, 130, 132, 165, 178
   Church of St-Honoré 58
   Church of St-Martin 58
   Church of St-Solenne, cathedral 58
   Hôtel d'Alluye 56, 97
   Hôtel de Jassaud 91
   Hôtel Salviati 98
   rue Fontaine-des-Élus 91
   rue Pierre de Blois 91
   rue Porte Chartraine 132
   rue Saint-Honoré 91
   suburb of Le Foix 58
   suburb of Vienne 58
Blois, château de 8–9, 21, 25, 39, 56–59, 68–69, 71, 79,
   82, 90, 107–109, 129–133, 136, 140, 142, 154, 157, 159,
   164, 174–175, 177
   Louis XII wing 25, 56, 68, 71, 90, 130, 157, 159
   François I wing 21, 79, 82, 109, 132, 136, 140, 142,
    154–155, 157, 174–175, 177
   Chapelle de Saint-Calais 58
   Collegiate church of Saint-Sauveur 58
   Galerie des Cerfs 58
   Pavilion of Anne de Bretagne 76
   Tour de Châtellerault 39

BOHIER, family 39, 90–91
   Thomas (d. 1524) 87, 89–90, 105
BOIS-JOURDAIN, Janet du, seigneur d'Azay 105
BONAPARTE, Louis-Eugène, the Prince Imperial
   (1856–1879) 164
BONAPARTE, Napoleon (1769–1821) 165
BONNIVET, Admiral de (see Gouffier de Bonnivet)
Bonnivet, château de (Vendeuvre, Vienne) 91, 129–132,
   145
BOURBON, Louis-Henri, duc de (1692–1740) 163
Bourges (Cher) 36, 55, 87, 92–93, 131
   Hôtel Jacques Coeur 92–93
Bourges, château de 39, 55
Bourgueil (Indre-et-Loire) 15
BOURRÉ, Guillaume, father of Jean Bourré 88
   Jean 48, 88–89
Bourré (Loir-et-Cher) 8, 23
BOUTELOUP, Guillaume 58
BRAMANTE, Donato d'Angelo Lazzari (1444–1514) 57
BRANTÔME, Pierre de Bourdeilles, seigneur de
   (c. 1540–1614) 57
   Vie des Dames illustres 76
   Vie des Hommes illustres et des Grands Capitaines
   français 85
Bréhémont (Indre-et-Loire) 11
Bretagne 7, 87
BRIÇONNET, family 29, 88, 91, 105
   Guillaume (d. 1514), cardinal (1495), bishop of
   Saint-Malo, father of Catherine Briçonnet 105
   Catherine (d. 1528), wife of Thomas Bohier 105
BRIDORÉ (see Bastarnay, Imbert de, seigneur
   de Bridoré)
BRILLAC, family de 95
   Charles de (d. 1509) 90, 95
BRIOSCO, Andrea, called "Il Riccio" (1470–1532) 150
Brittany (see Bretagne)
BRIZAY, Jacques de 139
BROGLIE, family de 164
   Amédée, prince de 163
BUEIL, Jean V de (d. 1477) 32
Burgundy 55, 87
Bury, château de (Molineuf, Loir-et-Cher) 38, 56, 59,
   87, 91, 96, 108, 129–130, 133

C

Cambrai (Nord) 108
CATHERINE DE MÉDICIS (1519–1589), wife of
   Henri II 39
Challain-La-Potherie, château de (Maine-et-Loire) 161,
   167
Chambord, château de (Loir-et-Cher) 7–8, 23, 35–36,
   38–39, 57–59, 84–85, 91, 107, 129–130, 132–133,
   146–149, 151–153, 159, 164–165, 178, 180–181
   Donjon 146–147, 149, 151–153
Chambord, park 19, 58, 165
CHAMBRAY, family de 144
CHARLES VII (1403–1461), King of France (1422)
   35–36, 55, 65, 87, 91, 105
CHARLES VIII (1470–1498), King of France (1483)
   8–9, 56, 65–67, 72–73, 81, 89–90, 105
CHARLES D'ORLÉANS (see Orléans)
CHARLES V (1500–1558), Holy Roman Emperor (1519)
   59
CHARLES THE BOLD, duc de Bourgogne (1433–1477)
   55, 57
CHÂTEAUBRIAND, François René, vicomte de
   (1768–1848)
   Vie de Rancé, 1844 180
Châteaudun, château de (Eure-et-Loir) 36, 38, 41, 46,
   52, 55, 75, 132, 140, 142
   Wing Dunois 75, 140
   Wing Longueville 140, 142
Château-Gontier (Mayenne) 88
Chaumont-sur-Loire (Loir-et-Cher) 39, 163

Chaumont, château de 7, 13, 39, 46, 51–52, 59, 130,
   163–164, 172, 173
   Tour d'Amboise 39, 46
Cheillé (Indre-et-Loire) 35
Chenonceaux, château de (Indre-et-Loire) 39, 47, 87,
   89–90, 105–106, 109, 129–130, 132–133, 162–163, 170,
   171
   Bohier building 171
   "Tour des Marques" 47
Cher, river 7–9, 14, 59, 170–171
CHEVALIER, Bernard 88–89
Cheverny, château de (Loir-et-Cher) 59
Chinon (Indre-et-Loire) 8–9, 16–17, 35, 38, 105
Chinon, château de 7, 35–36, 40, 44, 59
   Tour de Boisy 44
   Donjon du Coudray 44
   Fort du Coudray 44
   Tour du Moulin 44
CLAUDE DE FRANCE (1499–1524), wife of François I
   9, 39, 58–59, 64, 69–70
COEUR, Jacques (1395–1456) 8, 87–88, 131
   Pierre, father of Jacques Coeur 87
Cologne 108
COMMYNES, Philippe de, seigneur d'Argenton
   (1447?–1511)
   Mémoires, 1498 63, 66
CORTONE, Dominique de (d. c. 1549) 58
Cosson, river 7, 84, 178, 180–181
COTTEREAU, Guillaume 91
Coudray-Montpensier (le), château du (Seuilly,
   Indre-et-Loire) 32
COURAJOD, Louis (1841–1896) 165
COURIER, Paul-Louis (1772–1825) 165
CROIX, Jean de la 106

D

DAILLON, Jacques de (d. 1525) 134
   Jean de, father of Jacques de Daillon 134
DELORME (DE L'ORME), Philibert (1515–1570)
   Le Premier tome de l'Architecture, 1567 132–133
DEROY, Isidore Laurent (1797–1886) 162
   La Loire et ses bords, 1849 164
   Vues pittoresques des châteaux de France, 1830 168
DIANE DE POITIERS, duchesse de Valentinois
   (1499–1566) 39, 52, 171
Digoin (Saône-et-Loire) 7
DINTEVILLE, Jacques de (d. 1506) 58
DION, Roger 8
Disneyland 161
DOULCET, François 91
DREUX BRÉZÉ, Scipion, marquis de (1793–1845) 161
DUBAN, Jacques Félix (1797–1870) 174, 177
DU CERCEAU, Jacques Androuet (c. 1510–c. 1585) 58
   Les plus Excellents Bastiments de France, 1576–1579 80,
   84, 96
DUCOS, Roger (1747–1816) 164
DUNOIS, Jean d'Orléans, comte de (c. 1403–1468),
   father of François I de Longueville 36, 41, 52
DUPIN, Claude (1684–1769) 163
   Madame, née Fontaine (1706–1795), wife of Claude
   Dupin 163
DUPLESSIS-MORNAY (see Mornay, Philippe de)
DUPRAT, Antoine (1463–1535), cardinal 90
DUSSILLON, Charles-Henri (d. c. 1860) 162, 168
DU THIER, Jean, seigneur de Ménars (d. 1559) 130

E

Echo, nymphe 15
Ecouen, château d' (Val d'Oise) 132
   Musée de la Renaissance d' 77–78
Empire, Holy Roman (962–1806) 59, 90, 129, 133
Empire, First (1804–1814) 164
Empire, Second (1848–1870) 165
England 57

ERASMUS of Rotterdam (c. 1469–1536) 57
ESPINAY, family d' 32
ESTAMPES DE VALENÇAY, Jacques d' (b. 1518) 134
    Louis d', father of Jacques 134
EUDES, seigneur de Blois 35
Europe 88, 107

F

FALLOUX, Frédéric, comte de (1811–1886) 161
Feudalism 161
Field of the Cloth of Gold (1520) 59, 90
Flanders 56–57, 66, 133
FLAUBERT, Gustave (1821–1880)
    Par les champs et les grèves, Touraine et Bretagne, 1847
    170, 175
FOIX, Odet comte de, seigneur de, Lautrec (d. 1528),
    maréchal de France 107
Fontainebleau, château de (Seine-et-Marne) 88
Fontevrault, abbey of (Maine-et-Loire) 132
Fougères-sur-Bièvre, château de (Loir-et-Cher) 8, 19,
    21, 25, 52, 59, 75, 91, 94
FOULQUES III NERRA (972–c. 1040), seigneur
    d'Anjou (987) 35, 43
FOUQUET (FOUCQUET), Nicolas, vicomte de Vaux,
    marquis de Belle-Isle (1615–1680) 88
France 7, 9, 11, 27, 31, 33, 35, 55–58, 64, 66, 81, 87, 89,
    93, 105, 129, 132–133, 161–163, 165, 169
Franche-Comté 55
FRANÇOIS I (1494–1547), King of France (1515) 7, 9,
    23, 37, 39, 55–59, 84, 88, 90, 105, 107–108, 129, 132
Frankfurt, diet of 90
Frapesle (Indre-et-Loire) 16
FUMÉE, family 105
    Adam 105

G

Gaillon, château de (Eure) 90, 109, 129–130, 133
GEBELIN, François 131, 165
Geneva 87
Genoa 68, 90
GEYMÜLLER, Heinrich, baron de (1839–1909) 165
GIÉ, Pierre de Rohan, sire de (1451–1513), maréchal de
    France 29, 58–59, 90
GILLONET, Denis 106
GOUFFIER DE BONNIVET, Guillaume (d. 1525),
    admiral 90, 107, 131
Grandmont (Indre-et-Loire) 35
Gué-Pan (Le), château du (Monthou-sur-Cher, Loir-et-
    Cher) 87, 130
Guerre du Bien Public 88
Guerre folle 56
GUILLAUME, Jean 108, 129, 132

H

HARDION, Jean-Marie Louis (b. 1858) 107, 112, 115,
    118, 120, 124, 163
HENRI II PLANTAGENET (1133–1189), King of
    England (1154) 8, 40
HENRI II (1519–1559), King of France (1547) 91, 132
HENRI III (1551–1589), King of France (1574) 175
HENRI IV (1553–1610), King of Navarre (1562) and
    France (1589) 162–163, 169, 172
HENRI VIII (1491–1547), King of England and
    Ireland (1509) 57
Herbault-en-Sologne, château d' (Neuvy, Loir-et-Cher)
    59, 91
HODÉ, René (1840–1870) 161, 167
HUGO, Victor (1802–1885)
    En Voyage, Alpes et Pyrénées, 1843 22
Hundred Days, the (20 March 1815–8 July 1815) 162
Hundred Years War 35–36, 88
HURAULT, Jacques, seigneur de Cheverny (d. 1519),
    father of Jean I Hurault 136
HURAULT, Jean I (1480–1541) 136

I

Ile-Bouchard (Indre-et-Loire) 7, 17
Indre, river 7–9, 16–17, 37, 39, 106, 111
Islette (L'), château de (Cheillé, Indre-et-Loire) 39,
    130, 134
Italy 7, 9, 27, 55–57, 59, 66, 87, 90–91, 105, 108, 129,
    133, 151, 165

J

JASON 24
JOAN OF ARC, St, "the Maid of Orléans"
    (1412–1431) 35
Josselin, château de (Pontivy, Morbihan) 132–133, 145

K

KAPURTHALA, maharajah of 164
Kashmir 178

L

LA GUERTIÈRE (GUESTIÈRE), François de
    (b. 1624) 131
LA MORANDIÈRE, Jules de (1813–1883) 164, 173
Langeais, château de (Indre-et-Loire) 35, 89, 161
Languedoc 91
Langue d'Oïl 91
LA POINTE, François de (active 1666–1690) 131
Launay, manoir of (Villebernier, Maine-et-Loire) 56,
    60–61
LAUTREC (see Foix, Odet comte de)
LE BRETON, Jean 80
Légion d'Honneur, Ordre de la 165
LÉONARDO DA VINCI (1452–1519) 7, 59, 129–130,
    132, 147–148
LESBAHY, Antoine, father of Philippe Lesbahy 105
    Philippe, wife of Gilles Berthelot 105–108, 133
LIMBOURG, Pol de (active in the service of Jean de
    Berry from 1411– d. c. 1416)
    Les Très Riches Heures du Duc de Berry, c. 1415 36
LIPPOMANO, Jérôme
    Voyage de Jérôme Lippomano …, 1577 31
Loches (Indre-et-Loire) 8, 102
    Porte Picois 102
Loches, château de 35–36, 43, 45, 55, 59, 64–65, 69
    Agnès Sorel Tower 65
Loir, river 14, 41
Loire, river 7–9, 11–12, 16, 22, 24, 33, 35–37, 39, 41, 45,
    55–56, 59, 67, 73, 83, 85, 88, 91, 103, 107–109, 119,
    129, 131–133, 156, 161–163, 165, 173, 178
Loire, Valley of the 7–9, 35, 59, 101, 129–130
LOMBARDO, Cristoforo 150
LONGUEVILLE, François I de, father of François II 41,
    52
    François II de (d. 1513) 41, 52
Loudun (Vienne) 105
LOUIS I, comte de and then duc d'Anjou (1360–1384),
    King of Sicily and comte de Provence (1383) 13, 32
LOUIS XI (1423–1483), King of France (1461) 8–9, 36,
    55–57, 62, 88–89, 91, 105, 161, 169
LOUIS XII (1462–1515), King of France (1498) 8, 37,
    39, 55–59, 65, 68, 70, 75, 83, 88, 90–91, 105, 159
LOUIS XIV (1638–1715), King of France (1643) 88, 163
LOUIS XVI (1754–1793), King of France (1774–1791)
    162, 164
LOUIS-HENRI, duc de Bourbon (see Bourbon)
LOUIS-PHILIPPE I, duc d'Orléans (1773–1850), King of
    France (1830–1848) 164
LOUIS D'ORLÉANS (see Orléans)
LOUISE DE SAVOIE (1476–1531), regent of France
    (1515 and 1525), mother of François I 107
LOYSEAU, Charles (1566–1627)
    Traité des Seigneuries, 1608 37
Lude (Le), château du (Sarthe) 39, 109, 134, 139, 155
Lye (Indre) 8

Lyon (Rhône) 7, 59, 64, 81
Lyré, today Liré (Maine-et-Loire) 24

M

MACHIAVEL, Nicolò Machiavelli (1469–1527) 55, 57
  Il Principe, 1512 (published 1531) 55, 57
Mâcon (Saône-et-Loire) 7
MAILLÉ, René, comte de (d. 1531) 134
Maine 55
MANUZIO, Aldo, Manuzio (c. 1449–1515) 133
MARCASSEAU, Jean 106
MARIE DE CLÈVES (1426–1487), princess of the house
  La Marck, wife of Charles I, duc d'Orléans 91
MARY TUDOR (1516–1558), Queen of England and
  Ireland (1553) 91
Marignano, battle of (1515) 90
MAROT, Jean des Mares or des Marets (1463–c. 1526)
  Le Voyage de Gênes, 1507 68, 76
MARQUES, Jean II 47
MAUGENDRE, Adolphe (1809–1895) 167
MAUPOINT, Pierre 106–107
MAYAUD 161
Mediterranean 7, 87
Mehun-sur-Yèvre, château de (Cher) 36–37
Meillant, château de (Cher) 109, 132–133
MENIER, Gaston 163
Menier, factory (Seine-et-Marne) 171
Ménitré (La), manor of La (Maine-et-Loire) 56, 60
Metz (Moselle) 108
MICHELANGELO, Buonarroti (1475–1564) 91
Middle Ages 132, 165
Milan 8, 58–59, 90, 105, 129–130
Montbazon (Indre-et-Loire) 16
Montbazon, château de 7, 35
MONTFAUCON, P. Bernard de (1655–1741)
  Les Monumens de la monarchie française…, 1729–1733
  75
Montfrault, pavilion of (Loir-et-Cher) 59
Montils (les), (see Plessis-lès-Tours)
MONTMORENCY-TANCARVILLE, prince de 163
Montpellier (Hérault) 87
Montpoupon, château de (Ceré-la-Ronde, Indre-et-
  Loire) 30
Montrésor, château de (Indre-et-Loire) 7, 30
Montrichard (Loir-et-Cher) 14
Montrichard, château de 7, 35, 43, 59
MORNAY, Philippe de, seigneur de Plessis-Marly,
  usually known as Duplessis-Mornay (1549–1623) 13
Mortier-Crolles, château de (Craon, Mayenne) 29, 90
MORVILLIERS, family de 91
MOULIN, Philippe du (d. 1506) 26, 48, 50
Moulin (Le), château du (Lassay-sur-Croisne,
  Loir-et-Cher) 26, 48, 50, 129
Moulins (Allier) 87

N

Nantes (Loire-Atlantique) 7–8, 31
Nantes, château de 36, 55, 132
Naples 66, 90, 129
Naples, kingdom of (Angevin dynasty: 1266–1442) 36,
  56
NAVAGERO, Andrea
  Voyage d'André Navagero en Espagne et en France…,
  1528 18, 83
Nîmes (Gard) 87
Noisiel-sur-Marne (Seine-et-Marne) 170
Normandy 89–90, 105

O

ORLÉANS, family d' 164
  Charles duc d' (1394–1465), father of Louis XII 10, 56
  Louis duc d' (see Louis XII)
  Philippe duc d' (1674–1723), regent of France
    (1715–1723) 164

Adelaïde de Bourbon, duchesse d' (d. 1821), mother of
  Louis-Philippe 164
Orléans (Loiret) 7–10, 57, 91
Outre-Seine-et-Yonne 91

P

PACELLO DA MERCOGLIANO (d. 1534) 9, 58, 67
PALUSTRE, Léon (1838–1894) 165
Paris 7, 35–36, 59, 88, 105–107, 161, 163
  Comédie française 164
  Hôtel royal des Tournelles 59
  Musée de Cluny 30, 32
  Palais du Louvre 39, 132
  Palais des Tuileries 162
  Opéra 164
Pavia 107, 129, 151, 161
Pavia, Charterhouse of 133, 150–151
PELOUZE, Madame 163
PENSÉE, Charles François Joseph (1799–1871) 178
Péronne (Somme) 57
PHELIPPEAUX, family 91
PHILIP I THE FAIR (1478–1506), Archduke of
  Austria, governor of the Netherlands (1495) 57
PHILIPPE II AUGUSTE (1165–1223), King of France
  (1179) 44
PHILIP OF AUSTRIA (see Philip I the Fair)
Picardie 55
Pierrefonds, château de (Oise) 161
Plessis-Bourré (Le), château du (Cheffes, Maine-et-
  Loire) 37, 48, 88, 130, 161
Plessis du Parc lez Tours (see Plessis-lès-Tours)
Plessis-lès-Tours (Le), château du (La Riche, suburb of
  Tours, Indre-et-Loire) 36, 55, 58–59, 62–63
Poitou 91
Poncé-sur-le-Loir, château de (Sarthe) 132, 144–145
Pont-de-Ruan (Indre-et-Loire) 17
Port-Huault, ford of (Indre-et-Loire) 35
PRIE, family de 30
PRINCE IMPERIAL (see Bonaparte, Louis-Eugène)
Provence 55
Provence, kingdom of 36, 56

Q

Quakers 165
QUATREBARBES, Théodore, comte de (1807–1871)
  161

R

RABELAIS, François (1494–1553) 9
RAFFIN, Antoine 108
Réaux (Les), château de (Chouzé-sur-Loire, Indre-et-
  Loire) 29
REFUGE, Pierre de (d. 1497) 19, 21, 25, 52, 75, 91, 94
Renaissance 7, 12, 27, 39, 50, 57, 87–88, 91, 129–130,
  132, 140, 142, 161–162, 165, 169, 180
RENÉ I THE GOOD (1409–1480), duc d'Anjou, comte
  de Provence, King of Naples (1438–1442) and titular
  King of Sicily (1434–1480) 36, 39, 55–56, 58, 60–61
  Le Mortifiement de Vaine Plaisance, c. 1458 61
Republic, Second (1848–1852) 164
Republic, Third (1870–1940) 163–164
Restoration 161–162, 164
Revolution, French (1789–1799) 162, 165
Rhine, valley of the 56
Rigny-Ussé (Indre-et-Loire) 17
Rivarennes (Indre-et-Loire) 35
Roanne (Loire) 7–8, 59, 87
ROBERTET, Florimond, baron d'Alluye (d. 1522) 38,
  56, 59, 87–88, 91, 96–97
ROCHEFOUCAULD BOYERS, François de la 161
Roches-Tranchelion (Les), château des (Avon-les-
  Roches, Indre-et-Loire) 36
Roches-Tranchelion (Les), church of (Indre-et-Loire)
  133

Roguet, Félix (1822–1888) **163, 171**
Rohan, Pierre de (see Gié, sire de)
Romorantin-Lanthenay (Loir-et-Cher) **7, 129**
Romorantin, château de **129**
Ronsard, Pierre de (1524–1585) **37**
   Les Amours, 1553 **15**
   Élégie sur la forêt de Gastine, 1584 **20**
Rousseau, Etienne **106**
Rousseau, Jean-Jacques (1712–1778) **163**
Rousseau, Pierre **106**
Royat (Puy-de-Dôme) **38**
Ruzé, family **105**
   Jeanne, wife of Jacques de Beaune, seigneur de
   Semblançay **105**

S

Saché (Indre-et-Loire) **16–17**
Saint-Aignan (Loir-et-Cher) **8, 14**
St-Cyr, Guillaume Artault, abbé de (see Artault,
   Guillaume)
St-Michel, Order of **89**
Sainte-Maure, plateau of **9**
Salle, Étienne de la **58**
Salviati, Bernard, father of Cassandre Salviati **37,
   52, 94**
Sanson, Paul-Ernest (1836–1918) **173**
Saône, river **7**
Sauldre, river **7**
Saulnier, Jules (1817–1881) **170**
Saumur (Maine-et-Loire) **23, 56, 91, 102**
Saumur, château de **8, 13, 36**
Saxe, Maurice, comte de (1696–1750), maréchal de
   France **165**
Say, family **163**
   Marie **163**
Semblançay (see Beaune)
Semblançay, château de (Indre-et-Loire) **44, 87**
Seuilly (Indre-et-Loire) **32**
Seyssel, Claude de (1450–1520)
   La Grande Monarchie de France, 1519 **57**
Silvestre, Israël (1621–1691) **90**
Sourdeau, Jacques (d. 1522) **58**
Spain **57**
Stendhal, Henri Beyle, dit (1783–1842)
   Mémoires d'un touriste, 1838 **12**
Strabo, geographer (c. 58 BC–c. 25 AD) **7**

T

Talcy, château de (Loir-et-Cher) **37, 52, 94**
Tarascon (Bouches-du-Rhône) **39**
Tassin, Nicolas
   *Plans et profils de toutes les principales villes … de
   France,* 1631 **8, 9, 11**
Thibaut (Thibaud) I le Tricheur, comte de
   Blois (c. 908–c. 978) **35, 40**
Thibaut (Thibaud) V the Good, comte de Blois
   and Chartres (d. 1191) **46**
Thoreau le Maroy **106**

Thoreau, Jacques **106**
Tiber, river **24**
Touraine **7–9, 31, 33, 35–36, 38, 42, 55, 88, 129, 161**
Tours (Indre-et-Loire) **8–9, 11, 22, 26, 35–36, 55–56,
   62, 70, 88, 91, 98–100, 105–107, 109, 165**
   Cathedral of Saint-Martin **91**
   Cloisters of collegiate church of St Martin **98**
   Fontaine de Beaune **91**
   Hôtel de Beaune-Semblançay **98–99**
   Hôtel Goüin **91, 100, 109**
   Hôtel de la Petite Bourdaisière **26, 55, 62**
   rue Bouchereau **91**
   rue du Change **91**
   rue Colbert **91**
   rue du Commerce **91**
   rue de la Monnaie **91**
   rue Nationale **91**
Trélazé (Maine-et-Loire) **8**
Trèves-Cunault (Maine-et-Loire) **23**
Trojan War **57**
Turmeau, Étienne **106**
Turpenay (Indre-et-Loire) **35**

U

Ulysses, legendary King of Ithaca **24**
Union Générale, bank **163–164**
Ussé, château d' (Rigny-Ussé, Indre-et-Loire) **7, 32, 39,
   130, 133, 155**
   Chapel of collegiate church **133, 155**

V

Vachon, Marius (1850–1928) **165**
Valençay, château de (Indre) **39, 109, 134, 136, 157**
Vendôme (Loir-et-Cher) **14**
Venice **59, 129, 180**
Verger (Le), château du (Marne-et-Loire) **90, 129–130**
Veuil, château de (Indre) **136**
Vienne, river **7–9, 17, 40**
Vigny, Alfred, comte de (1797–1863)
   Cinq-Mars ou une conjuration sous Louis XIII, 1826 **33,
   172, 178**
Villandry, château de (Indre-et-Loire) **80**
Villebrême, secretary to Marie de Clèves **91**
Villegongis, château de (Indre) **37, 39, 130, 139, 158**
Villesavin, château de (Tour-en-Sologne, Loir-et-Cher)
   130
Vinci (see Leonardo da)
Viollet-le-Duc, Eugène Emmanuel
   (1814–1879)
   Dictionnaire raisonné de l'Architecture française …
   1854–1868 **38–39**
   Entretiens sur l'architecture …, 1872 **27**
Vitry, Paul (1872–1945) **91**

W

Wars of Religion **35, 38**
Waterloo, battle of (1815) **162**
World War I **163**

ILLUSTRATIONS

© All the views of sites and buildings are original photographs taken by Michel Saudan and Lionel Saudan (illustrations on pp. 26 above, 50 above, 100 above, 138, 160, 170 below and 173 below)

Frontispieces to chapters

The Loire
View of the right bank near Varennes-sur-Loire **6**

Loches (Indre-sur-Loire)
Château, fortress rebuilt in the 11th century; royal apartments completed second half of the 16th century:
11th-century keep, north-west façade **34**

Chambord (Loir-et-Cher)
Château, begun 1519 for François I; work completed late 17th century:
View of the park with the deer-ponds **54**

Bourges (Cher)
Hôtel Jacques Coeur, rue Jacques Coeur, built 1443–1450:
Detail of the street façade **86**

Azay-le-Rideau (Indre-et-Loire)
Château, built 1518–1527 for Gilles Berthelot:
North face, view from the drive leading to the château, west wing and north façade of the main building **104**
North-west face, view from an arm of the Indre: west wing and tower replacing the former keep **160**

Chenonceaux (Loir-et-Cher)
Château, built 1515–1522 for Thomas Bohier; bridge and great hall on the Cher 1556, architect Philibert Delorme; gallery on the Cher 1570–1576:
East view, the Bohier building and the beginning of the gallery **128**

Places illustrated

Amboise (Indre-et-Loire)
Manor of Le Clos-Lucé (until the 17th century the manor of Le Cloux), built 1477 for Étienne le Loup; home of Leonardo da Vinci 1516–1519:
Post and beam of the gallery **19**

Château, the old fortress rebuilt for Hugues I d'Amboise 1115; reversion of the seigneurie of Amboise to the crown 1431; rebuilding of the château 1491 to post-1515:
View from the banks of the Loire **66**

Royal apartments, Charles VIII wing 1491–1498, Tour des Minimes 1495–1498:
Royal apartments, Charles VIII wing **66**
Terrace, gardens originally designed by Pacello da Mercogliano **67**
Royal apartments and gallery joining them to the "apartments of the royal children" (now destroyed) **67**
Ramp inside the Tour des Minimes **72**
Access to the château terrace **72**
Covered gallery looking out on the Loire **73**

The Chapelle St-Hubert, 1491–1496:
Vault of the chapel **77**

Argy (Indre)
Château, rebuilt for the de Brillac family mid-14th century; residence of Charles de Brillac pre-1509:
Galleries, north and west wings **95**

Azay-le-Rideau (Indre-et-Loire)
Château, built 1518–1527 for Gilles Berthelot:
Approach to the château, looking towards the axis of the great staircase **111**

Façades and turrets:
Capital of a pilaster, north façade **108**
View of the east façade **113**
West façade **114**
South façade **115**
South façade, details **116–117**
Turret at the south-west corner **112**
South-east angle turret, detail **116**
South-west angle turret, cul-de-lampe **117**

Great staircase, north façade:
Ermine of Claude of France on a window base **58**
Canopied niches, details of ornamentation **118–119**
Double windows on the first floor **118**
View looking up at the staircase façade **119**

Great staircase, interior:
Detail of handrail **120**
Vaulted ceiling on 4th landing of the staircase **120**
First flight of the staircase **121**

Doors:
Doorway to stair of the keep **122**
Doors leading to the great staircase **122**
Door in the west façade, overlooking the moat **123**
Door in the east façade, opening out to the courtyard **123**

Dormer windows:
Dormer of the great staircase: north façade **124**
Dormer in the west façade **125**
East façade, right wing **158**

Roofs:
West roof, with chimneys **25**
Finials of the roof **126**
South-east angle turret, details of the roof **127**

Restored from 1845 onwards for Antoine Marie de Biencourt and his son Armand de Biencourt, architect Charles Dussillon:
View from the "English-style" park **168**
View of the north tower, replacing the old keep, 1854 **169**

Baugé (Maine-et-Loire)
Manor, restored for René d'Anjou from 1455:
Manor de Baugé, begun 1455 **60**

Beaugency (Loiret)
Hôtel de Ville, begun 1525, building attributed to Pierre Briart:
Street façade:
First-floor windows **102**
Entrance porch **103**

Blois (Loir-et-Cher)
Château of the comtes de Blois, which became a royal residence in 1498:
Roofs of the town, seen from the terrace 24
Terrace with fountain, early 16th century, formerly in the château gardens 82
Louis XII wing, 1498–1504:
Façade overlooking the forecourt:
Porcupine of Louis XII 56
Gargoyle on the cornice of the forecourt façade 68
Entrance with equestrian statue of Louis XII (copy dating from 1857) 69
State courtyard and gallery:
Dormer window 25
View of the state courtyard 70
Window, arcades, and foot of the state staircase 71
Detail of cornice 157
Roof overlooking the courtyard; dormer with monogram of Louis XII 158
François I wing, 1515–pre-1524:
Roof trusses; timber roof structures in the shape of an upturned hull 21
Hall on first floor:
Tympanum of doorway 78
Ornamental mantelpiece with the royal emblem 79
Façade overlooking the courtyard:
Detail of façade 136
Detail of cornice 156
Staircase, 1519–1520, master mason Jacques Sourdeau (?):
Staircase 141
Ribbed vault rising from the newel 142
Detail of the balustrade of the spiral staircase 142
Ornamentation of the base 82–83
Medallion on the base of the staircase 154
Restoration, 1845–1860, architect Félix Duban:
François I wing, façade of the loggias:
View of part of the restored façade 174
View of the échauguette 177
Pavilion of Anne de Bretagne, built between 1499 and 1515, formerly surrounded by the gardens of the château:
The queen's monogram 76
Hôtel d'Alluye, 8 rue St-Honoré, built 1508 for Florimond Robertet, baron d'Alluye:
Interior courtyard and galleries 96–97
Bay window in the east wing 97
Hôtel Salviati, 5 rue du Puits-Chastel, late 15th century:
Loggia overlooking the courtyard 98

Bourges (Cher)
Hôtel Jacques Coeur, rue Jacques Coeur, built 1443–1450, master mason Colin le Picart:
Tympanum of door on the north staircase, overlooking the courtyard 92
Decorated window bases, main staircase overlooking the courtyard 92–93
Interior courtyard and open gallery 93

Bourré (Loir-et-Cher)
Old limestone quarry 22

Challain-la-Potherie (Maine-et-Loire)
Château, built 1848 for Comte François de La Rochefoucauld Boyers, architect René Hodé:
Bridge leading to the château 166
Views from the river running past the park 166–167

Chambord (Loir-et-Cher)
Chambord park
Forest in autumn 18
Château, begun 1519, originally for François I; the keep, 1519–1539; east and west wing, 1538–1552; west wing (Henri II wing), three lower-built wings for

household offices, and Porte Royale completed late 17th century; gardens and canalization of the river Cosson late 18th century:
View of the château and the Cosson canal 84
South-east view, the Porte Royale side 178
North-west view, the garden side 179
View of the park 180
View of the Cosson canal 181
The keep:
Terrace of the keep 85
North-west façade 151
North-west roof 159
Staircase of the keep, after an idea by Leonardo da Vinci:
Capitals of the staircase, c. 1530 146
Guardroom and double spiral staircases 146–147
View of staircase, seen from blow 148
Lantern tower, seen from the terrace 149
Ornamentation:
Guardroom:
Volute corbel 23
Salamander of François I 57
West terrace and roof:
Corner capitals 152
Scroll of dormer 152
Culs-de-lampe 152–153

Châteaudun (Eure-et-Loire)
Château, keep built last third of the 12th century for Thibaut V; Dunois wing built 1459–1469 for Jean d'Orléans, comte de Dunois; further building 1500–1513 for François I and François II de Longueville; building completed 1532 (the Longueville wing):
North view from the banks of the Loir 41
Keep of Thibaut V 46
Parapet walk 52
Dunois wing:
Great hall and window embrasure 74
Kitchen 75
Gothic staircase 140
Longueville wing:
Renaissance staircase, 1511–1518:
Façade on the courtyard 140
Ribbed vault rising from the newel 142

Chaumont-sur-Loire (Loir-et-Cher)
Château de Chaumont, rebuilt 1465 for Pierre d'Amboise; work completed 1498–1510 for Charles II d'Amboise:
West wing 13
Tour d'Amboise, begun 1465 for Pierre d'Amboise 46
Entrance towers and drawbridge, 1498–1510:
Drawbridge and piers 50–51
View of the whole structure 51
Machicolations with emblems of Diane de Poitiers, restored c. 1560 52
Restoration 1847 onwards, architect Jules de La Morandière; restoration continued in 1878 by Paul-Ernest Sanson:
Stables, 1878 172
View of the château from the banks of the Loire 172
Cement bridge in the park, late 19th century 173

Chenonceaux (Loir-et-Cher)
Château, rebuilt c. 1515–1522 for Thomas Bohier; bridge and great hall on the Cher built 1556 for Diane de Poitiers, architect Philibert Delorme; gallery on the Cher built 1570–1576 for Catherine de Medici; restoration for Mme Pelouze, 1865, architect Félix Roguet:
Keep known as the "Tour des Marques", begun 1432 for Jean II Marques 47
West view from the left bank of the Cher 170
East view, from the gardens of Diane de Poitiers 171

Chinon (Indre-et-Loire)
Château, rebuilt for Thibaut le Tricheur, comte de
Blois, second half of the 10th century; reinforced by
Henry Plantagenet from 1160; fortifications reinforced
1205–1370 from the time of Philippe Auguste; royal
apartments completed in the 15th century:
Fortifications seen from the banks of the Vienne 40
*The Fort du Coudray, Tour du Moulin, Tour de Boisy
and Donjon du Coudray* 44

Le Coudray-Montpensier (Seuilly, Indre-et-Loire)
Château begun 1380 for Louis I, duc d'Anjou et de
Touraine; work completed late 15th century:
View from the hillsides of Seuilly 32

Fougères-sur-Bièvre (Loir-et-Cher)
Château, rebuilt 1475 for Pierre de Refuge; further
rebuilding 1510–1520 for Jean de Villebrême, grandson
of Pierre de Refuge:
Angle tower, timber structures of the turret 19
*Timber roof structures of the main building, in the shape
of an upturned hull* 20
Roof of the main building, with dormer window 25
North-east tower, machicolations on corbels 52
Guardroom 75
Gallery of interior courtyard, 1510–1520 94

The Indre
Between Saché and Pont-de-Ruan 16
Near Rigny-Ussé 17
Banks of the river Indre 110

Launay (Villebernier, Maine-et-Loire)
Manoir built pre-1480 for René d'Anjou:
Manoir de Launay 61

L'Islette (Cheillé, Indre-et-Loire)
Château, 1530–1531 for René de Maillé; completed
early 17th century for Charles de Maillé; roof modified
and dormers removed 1840:
South-west façade 134

Loches (Indre-et-Loire)
Château; fortress rebuilt in the 11th century; royal
apartments completed second half of the 16th century:
Keep built 11th century for Foulques Nerra:
Views of exterior and interior 42–43
Fortifications of the keep, 12th–13th century 45
Royal apartments:
Old Lodge, late 14th century, built for Charles VII
New Lodge, late 15th–early 16th century, built for
Charles VIII and Louis XII
Old Lodge and New Lodge 64
Interior courtyard in front of the royal apartments 65
Old Lodge and the Agnès Sorel Tower 65
Hôtel de Ville, 1535–1543:
*Façade in the place of the Hôtel de Ville, and the 15th-
century Picois gate* 102

The Loire
Embankment between Amboise and Tours 10
Former discharging wharf at Bréhémont 11

Le Lude (Sarthe)
Château, fortress rebuilt for Jean de Daillon from 1457;
1480–1533 turned into a château de plaisance for
Jacques de Daillon; 1787 building joining the north
wing (restored in the 19th century) and the south
wing:
South wing, 1520–1530, architect Jean Gendrot:
South building and angle towers 135
Window frame on angle tower 139
Façade of main building: window base 155

Mehun-sur-Yèvre (Cher)
Château, rebuilt 1367–1390 for Jean de Berry,
master mason Guy de Dammartin:
View from the old moat 37

Montpoupon (Céré-la-Ronde, Indre-et-Loire)
Château, begun 1320 for the de Prie family; work completed early 16th century:

Main building and entrance pavilion, early 16th century
30

Montrésor (Indre-et-Loire)
Château, fortress rebuilt in 1395 for Jean de Bueil;
seigneurial apartments built for Imbert de Bastarnay,
seigneur de Bridoré, 1493–late 16th century:
Seigneurial apartments, early 16th century 31

Montrichrad (Loir-et-Cher)
Bridge over the Cher, 13th or 14th century, restored
19th–20th century:
Bridge over the Cher 15

Château, begun 1120 for Hugues I d'Amboise:
Enceinte and keep 43

Mortier-Crolles (Craon, Mayenne)
Château, built late 15th century for Pierre de Rohan,
maréchal de Gié:
Towers of the fortress seen from the moat 28

Le Moulin (Lassay-sur-Croisne, Loir-et-Cher)
Château, built 1490–1506 for Philippe du Moulin;
restoration for M. de Marchéville 1910, architects
C.-L. Genuys and P. Chauvallon:
Detail of south-east façade of the main building 26
Lozenge and rectangle patterns on the south-west façade
27
*View from the north: the fortress and the main
building* 48
View from the east: the great tower 48
*Entrance bastion with gates for vehicles and
pedestrians* 50

Pavia (Lombardy)
The Charterhouse, founded 1396; church built
1433–1473, architects Giovanni Solari and sons; façade
1481–1499, architect Giovanni Antonio Amadeo,
sculptors Benedetto Briosco and Cristoforo Lombardo,
early sixteenth century:
Church, 1433–1473 150
Details of façade 150–151

Le Plessis-Bourré (Cheffes-sur-Sarthe, Maine-et-Loire)
Château, built for Jean Bourré 1468–1473:
View from the moat 49

Le Plessis-lès-Tours (Tours, La Riche, Indre-et-Loire)
Château, formerly manor of Les Montils; rebuilt for
Louis XI in 1474, restored for Charles VIII in 1505:
East wing, main building 62

Poncé-sur-le-Loir (Sarthe)
Château, built 1525–1535 for Jean IV and Jean V
de Chambray:
Interior of staircase, c. 1530:
Flight of steps with barrel vault 144–145
Detail of coffering in barrel vault 144–145

Les Réaux (Chouzé-sur-Loire, Indre-et-Loire)
Château, formerly Plessis-Rideau or Plessis-Macé
acquired by Guillaume Briçonnet 1495, west wing
built for Jean Briçonnet 1515–1559; east wing built for
Louis Taboureau early 18th century:
West wing:
Main building, with entrance towers and keep 29

Saint-Aignan (Loir-et-Cher)
Bridge over the Cher 14

Saumur (Maine-et-Loire)
Château, built late 14th century for Louis I, duc
d'Anjou; 15th century refurbished for René d'Anjou;
16th century fortified by Duplessis-Mornay:
Château de Saumur 12

Hôtel de Ville, 16th century:
Cul-de-lampe of an angle turret 23
Façade seen from the banks of the Loire 102

Semblançay (Indre-et-Loire)
Château, fortress rebuilt early 16th century for Jacques
de Beaune de Semblançay:
Enceinte and round towers 44

Talcy (Loir-et-Cher)
Château, built mid-15th century for the Simon family;
rebuilt from 1520 for Bernard Salviati; refurbished
1633–1643 for Isabelle Salviati:
*Square entrance tower: machicolations, crenels and
merlons* 53
Interior courtyard 94

Tours (Indre-et-Loire)
Hôtel de la Petite Bourdaisière, 7 rue des Ursulines,
built late 15th century for the Babou de la Bourdaisière
family:
Detail of brickwork 26
Main building and first-floor window 63
Hôtel de Beaune-Semblançay, Jardin de Beaune-
Semblançay; built 1506–1518 for Jacques de Beaune,
seigneur de Semblançay:
Details of the façade of the main building 99
Hôtel de Goüin, 25 rue du Commerce, late 15th–early
16th century:
South façade, c. 1510:
Entrance porch 100
Details decorated window bases 100–101
South façade, c. 1510 101

Trêves-Cunault (Maine-et-Loire)
Fortified farm:
Pendentive of the échauguette 23

Ussé (Rigny-Ussé, Indre-et-Loire)
Château, rebuilt for Jean V and Antoine de Bueil mid-
15th century; keep, south wing and part of east wing
built 1485–1535 for Jacques and Antoine d'Espinay;
work completed for the Bernin de Valentinay family in
1695:
View of the north façade 33
Chapel of collegiate church, 1523–1535:
Details of doorways:
Ornamentation of the tympanum 154
Impost capitals 155

Valençay (Indre)
Château, work begun 1520–1530 for Louis d'Estampes
de Valençay, including north-west tower and begin-
ning of west wing; north wing and entrance pavilion
built 1540–1579 for Jacques d'Estampes and his brother
Jean; west wing completed for Dominique d'Estampes
mid-17th century:
Entrance pavilion:
Façade overlooking the courtyard 134
Details of façade overlooking the courtyard 136
Details of cornice:
North wing, 1579: 157
Entrance pavilion 157

Vendôme (Loir-et-Cher)
Bridge over an arm of the Loir 14

Veuil (Indre)
Château, built early 16th century for Jacques Hurault,
seigneur de Cheverny; work completed 1519–1541 for
Jean I Hurault:
Angle tower of the main building 137

Vienne
Between l'Ile-Bouchard and Chinon 17

Villandry (Indre-et-Loire)
Gardens of the Château de Villandry, laid out from
1536 for Jean le Breton, restored 1906:
Kitchen garden 80–81

Villegongis (Indre)
Château, built 1531–1538 for Jacques de Brizay; roof
and dormer windows of the façade looking out on the
courtyard restored 18th century:
Main building and angle towers 138
Ornamentation on the façade 139
East roof 158

Drawings and engravings

Anonymous
*View of the town and château de Chinon in Touraine,
seen from the Vienne;* engraving, late 18th century;
Paris, Bibliothèque Nationale, Cabinet des estampes
(Photo: B.N.) 40
Chenonceaux, from the Side of the Château; wash draw-
ing, late 16th century; Paris, Bibliothèque Nationale,
Cabinet des estampes (Photo: B.N.) 89

Deroy, Isidore
Château de Chenonceaux; lithograph, 1844; Paris, Bib-
liothèque Nationale, Cabinet des estampes (Photo:
B.N.) 162

Duban, Félix
*Château de Blois, François I wing, façade of the loggias.
Elevation and projected restoration;* wash drawing with
water colour, 1844; Paris, Bibliothèque du Patrimoine
(Photos: Jean-Loup Charmet):
Elevation 175
Projected restoration 175
Projected restoration, detail 176

Hardion, Jean
*Château d'Azay-le-Rideau, elevations and projected
restoration;* wash drawings with water colour,
1904–1906; Paris, Bibliothèque du Patrimoine
(Photos: Jean-Loup Charmet):
*Plan showing situation of the town and
the château* 107
Ground-floor plan 112
South façade 115
North façade, the great staircase overlooking the courtyard
118
Section of the staircase with plans and details 120
Dormer of great staircase, south façade 124

La Guertière, François de
Château de Bonnivet (Vandeuvre, Vienne), built 1516
onwards for Admiral de Bonnivet, engraving by F.
de La Pointe after de La Guertière, late 17th century;
Paris, Bibliothèque Nationale, Cabinet des estampes
(Photo: B.N.) 131

Leonardo da Vinci
Sketch for a staircase, fortifications and a lantern tower;
pen drawing, between 1516 and 1519; Paris,
the Louvre, Cabinet des Dessins (Photo: Réunion des
Musées Nationaux) 148

Maugendre, Alphonse
*Château de Challain-la-Potherie: view of the façade
as seen from the park;* lithograph by A. Maugendre,
c. 1860; Paris, Bibliothèque Nationale, Cabinet des
estampes (Photo: B.N.) 166

Nodet, M.
Hôtel Salviati: Elevation of the façade; wash drawing,
late 19th century; Paris, Caisse Nationale des Monuments Historiques et des Sites (Photo: © Archives
photographiques, Paris SPADEM) 99

Pensée, Charles
Château de Chambord; lithograph, 1845; Paris, Bibliothèque Nationale, Cabinet des estampes (Photo: B.N.)
178

Sanson, Paul-Ernest
Château de Chaumont, View from the north; wash
drawing, 1878; Paris, Archives Nationales, Fonds Sanson
(Photo: Jean-Loup Charmet) 173

Silvestre, Israël
Perspective View of the Château du Verger in Anjou
(early 16th century for the maréchal de Gié); engraving, mid-17th century; Paris, Bibliothèque Nationale,
Cabinet des estampes (Photo: B.N.) 90

Tapestries

French tapestry of c. 1500; Paris, Musée de Cluny (Photos: Réunion des Musées Nationaux):
The Vintage 30
Return from the Hunt 32

Flemish tapestry of c. 1510–1515; Ecouen, Musée de la Renaissance (Photos: Réunion des Musées Nationaux): The Story of David and Bathsheba:
Queen Michol and the Lords on the Balcony 77
Lords and ladies 78

Illuminated works

Anjou, René d'
Mortifiement de Vaine Plaisance, c. 1458; Brussels, Bibliothèque Royale Albert I, manuscripts section (Photos: Bibliothèque Royale):
The King in his Study ... fol. 1, ro 60
Woman about to cross the Bridge, fol. 50 61
The Coachman driving the Queen, fol. 43 61

Limbourg, Pol de
Les Très Riches Heures du Duc de Berry, c. 1415; Chantilly, Musée Condé (Photo: Giraudon):
The Temptation of Christ (Château de Mehun-sur-Yèvre), fol. 161 vo 36

Marot, Jean
Le Voyage de Gênes, 1507; Paris, Bibliothèque Nationale, manuscripts department (Photos: B.N.):
The entry of Louis XII into Genoa, fol. 15 vo 68
The Book given by its Author to Queen Anne de Bretagne 76

Treatises and illustrated works

Daly, César
Encyclopédie d'Architecture, vol. III, 1874, Geneva, Bibliothèque Publique et Universitaire (Photo: François Martin):
The Menier factory at Noisiel-sur-Marne 1871–1872; architect, Jules Saulnier 170

Delorme (De l'Orme), Philibert
Le Premier tome de l'Architecture, 1567, Geneva, Bibliothèque Publique et Universitaire (Photos: François Martin):
The Bad Architect 132
The Good Architect 133

Deroy, Isidore
La Loire et ses bords, 1849, Paris, Bibliothèque Nationale, Cabinet des estampes (Photo: B.N.):
Château de Chaumont 164

Vues pittoresques des châteaux de France, 1830, Paris, Bibliothèque Nationale, Cabinet des estampes (Photo: B.N.):
The Château d'Azay-le-Rideau before 1845 168

Du Cerceau, Jacques Androuet
Les plus Excellents Bastiments de France, 1576–1579, Geneva, Bibliothèque Publique et Universitaire (Photos: François Martin):
Château d'Amboise 80
Chambord, south-east façade 84

Château de Bury (built 1511–1515 for Florimond Robertet):
Elevation of the entrance side 96

Montfaucon, P. Bernard de
Les Monuments de la monarchie française ..., 5 vols., 1729–1733, Paris, Bibliothèque Nationale, Cabinet des estampes (Photo: B.N.):
Louis XII surrounded by this lords 74

Tassin, Nicolas
Plans et profils de toutes les principales villes et lieux considérables de France, 1631, Geneva, Bibliothèque Publique et Universitaire (Photos: François Martin):
Amboise 8
Tours 9
Map of the course of the river Loire 10

Viollet-le-Duc, Eugène
Dictionnaire raisonné de l'Architecture française du XIe au XVIe siècle, 1854–1868, Geneva, private collection:
Machicolations of Royat church 38
Machicolations of King René's gate at Tarascon 39

Archival document

Château d'Azay-le-Rideau, page of account book for the building in 1518–1519; Tours, archives of the department of Loir-et-Cher. (Paris, Caisse Nationale des Monuments Historiques et des Sites. © Archives photographiques SPADEM) 106